Pacific Hopscotch

Pacific Hopscotch

BY

SISTER MARIA DEL REY

ILLUSTRATED

CHARLES SCRIBNER'S SONS, NEW YORK
CHARLES SCRIBNER'S SONS, LTD., LONDON
1951

TO OUR LADY

Contents

Illustrations

Scientific Methods Are New to China
Granny Brings Every Last Grandchild to See the Sisters

[Between Pages 70 and 71]

The Igorots Celebrate the Great Feasts of the Church by a Canyao
Christian Schools Will Save the Philippines From Communism
Igorot Women Find This the Easiest Way to Carry Produce to Market

[Between Pages 86 and 87]

Our Lady of Guam Reigns Undisputed
Landing on Koror in the Palaus
Palauan Children Crowd the Back Steps for a Religion Lesson
A Kerosene Lamp on the Dictionary Lights the Evening Classes
"Shake Hands and Make Up!"

[Between Pages 126 and 127]

The Trees at Ise, Japan's Most Sacred Spot
Haruko-San Was Easy to Make Friends With
The Temple Dancing Girls Were Formal and Aloof
Chopsticks and Boy-Size Appetites Soon Empty the Little Tin Lunchboxes
Waters of Baptism Bring Life to a Dying Soul
In the Quonset Convent on Guam, You Can't Surpass That Old Southe'n Hospitality
Starvation and Leprosy, the Age-Old Scourges of Mankind

[Between Pages 166 and 167]

Hawaiian Harmony—Composed of All Nations and Races
Her Cabbage Patch Isn't Worrying Grandma Suzuki in Hawaii
Filipino Workers in the Sugarcane Fields Like to Share Avocados with the Sisters
Hawaiian Schools Are a Cross-Section of the World
Geronimo, a Bad Heart Case, Wins the Game Every Time—Almost!

CHINA

1

Red Roads

WE were six squeezed together in the front seat as the truck, loaded with rice, slipped and slid in pitch darkness, down the steep mountainsides near Tung Shek, Kwantung. Rice trucks travel by night to avoid Communist troops which infest the roads. Sloshy mud and driving rain made this trip even more invigorating.

At one time, we took a long slide toward eternity—long enough to review in haste the thoughts, words, deeds and omissions of an imperfect life. At another, as we edged around a U-turn of cliff, I tried to help the driver cut the wheel more sharply and was peremptorily brushed off, as I should have been.

I was wedged at the left of the driver, trying to shrink myself together so that his muscular arms and shoulders could have free play to swing the wheel. On my other side, a nondescript little fellow clung with his elbows to the window-frame while his feet found precarious footing on the running board, hidden far under me. Like all trucks in China, the wooden box-car-like body had been built away out on either side over the chassis.

The ragged little man who clung on with one toe, was very important to us, however. He was the Block-Pusher-In. His duty was to drop off on hills and keep a triangular wooden block near the back wheel. If we started to slide back downhill, he wedged his block into the mud until the wheels got a grip on the road again. Several times, when we went to the very edge of the cliff, I thought this poor little fellow had dropped off into sheer space. But he always reappeared, puffing up to the front again, and, with a hop and skip, jumped onto the running board. His reward for such heroic action was a puff or two from the driver's cigarette. He would thrust his raggy coat sleeve across my face and take the cigarette from where it hung limp on the driver's lip. He took his puff and returned it to its rightful place. But the grand apologetic smile he gave me made up, and more, for his brushings.

Four other men sat on the driver's right. One of our Sisters was stowed up under the roof, her feet on a level with our shoulders. Our "boy," good Ah Min, was spread over the mud guard in front. Soaked, of course, but not noticing that. Many times, he was hanging over large amounts of nothing-at-all.

The five other Sisters inside the truck were really having a nice time. It was black and airless, of course, and the sacks of rice were musty, but rice is more amenable to the human frame than wood. The four hours or so passed quickly in cheerful conversation, interspersed with the rosary. One, who was weary indeed, lay back on the sacks and slept.

Even danger becomes monotonous; I was unable to gasp at any cliffs opening up ten feet ahead. Rather, in a dreamy sort of way, the eventful day passed in review.

We started out at 6:30 a.m. on the 52 mile drive, Kaying to Tung Shek, in the only private car in the diocese, the Bishop's aged but respectable station wagon.

At 9:00, a Communist soldier ran out of a wayside tea shop and pointed his rifle at us. Ah Min screeched the brakes, but our friend was mad. "You've got to stop when I aim my gun at you," he yelled.

Ah Min proffered a cigarette in the manner he has seen in the movies. "My friend, you do not know these foreign wagons. You cannot stop on a dime," he explained.

The Communist was not to be outdone in urbanity. "You may pass on, then," he said.

We thought we were through; this sort of thing had hap-

short gun they wear, hanging with the beads at their sides? (He meant our rosary crucifix.) Well, that's very powerful. Bandits don't dare oppose it. Even devils are afraid of that thing. All these people have to do is to touch it, and evils fall away from them."

As a rule in China, we do not talk to men on the road unless we are first spoken to. Our work is with women chiefly, and they themselves are most decorous in that regard. But here Sister could not resist smiling and giving them some idea of the real power of the crucifix.

A missioner travels by any means he can get, so long as it gets him where he must go.

This dictum has earned me many a narrow squeak, but perhaps no means of travel can cope with rear-wheel bicycle riding for thrills. Many missions are accessible only by walking or bicycles. Walking is easier on the nerves, but harder on the feet. After all, you cannot expect to walk 17 miles one day, and be ready for 20 the next day and 18 the day after. At least, not if you are a softie recently from America. Our Sisters do it now and then, but only after a year of breaking-in on shorter hikes.

With all the brash courage of comparative youth, I insisted that I could easily go around the Kaying missions by bicycle. I was not slow in boasting that 30 years ago, no kid in our block could touch me when it came to handlebar technique. Why, I could bicycle circles around these young Sisters!

"Thirty years ago, I think you said?" Sister Rita Marie inserted dubiously.

"A mere nothing in the light of eternity! I'm as fit today as I was then." And just to prove it I took out a bicycle and started around the narrow cement walks around the convent.

It went pretty well. My ego inflated enormously. A few wild gyrations of the front wheel, a sudden stop in a bramble bush, to be sure—but on the whole the old prowess was coming back.

Ah, pride. You know what it cometh before? All too true! Bishop Ford and Sister Rita Marie emerged from the convent and stood on the front steps finishing a discussion of mission

work. The black angel whose job it is to trick me into foolish-
ness whispered, "Sail past them now, and show them that 30
years is nothing in your young life."

Full speed ahead, I pedaled—easy, graceful command of
the wheel, perfect poise on the seat, no worries at all.

Then my good angel put a stone on the walk, to puncture
that pride. It worked. I tumbled, a heap of humility, at the
Bishop's feet. No bones broken, not even a bad bruise. Nothing
more was said, but we arranged to borrow the station wagon
from the good Maryknoll Fathers who lent it to us on any occasion, anyway.

From that time on, I rode bicycles only on the back seat,
which really isn't a seat at all, as I shall show you.

The best way to experience rear-wheel bicycling vicariously,
is to secure a bony horse (oh, a very bony horse) and put a
square block of wood on his aged rump. The block must not make
the slightest concession to the human frame—absolutely square.
Now, mount the square block on the bony rump and plant each
big toe on a tiny stirrup. Get someone to sit in front of you so
that your nose is right against his back. Now promise the beast,
"The best meal of your long-starved life awaits at the end of this
trail" and let him go to it with all the pent-up appetite the years
have stored in him.

You will be amazed how rock and rill fly past. Swaying
bamboo footbridges, threatening mountain chasms, shifting shale
pathways tilted to the abyss—a thousand spectacular deaths
mean nothing. The beast of iron and rubber skims along a ridge
in the rice paddies, while six feet below on either side mellifluous
mud awaits the slightest tremor of the wheel. You have nothing
to hold on to; every bump sets your nose and glasses in violent
collision with the perspiring shoulders before you. Your efforts
to steady yourself are frustrated. If you cling to the springs under
the driver's saddle, every jolt pinches your fingers. If you clench
your knees, you interfere with the pedaling; if you grip with
your heels, the back wheel scrapes your shoe. You learn, finally,
to hold on by sheer force of prayer.

Yet, no matter how wispy the driver, or decrepit the bike,

you always arrive at your destination, a little sore perhaps but safe.

The standard greeting between bike-men as they pass each other on the road, is a loud, "Is she heavy? She looks it!" There is never any doubt as to the answer. Nevertheless, they push along uphill until they can gasp no more before they ask you to walk to the top. On a jaunt of 17 miles one day, we got off 23 times. Sister Rita Marie said we walked "only a poulou (3⅓ miles)" but every inch of that poulou was standing on its ear.

The climbs were always worth it, though, as we mopped our steaming faces on the mountain top and viewed the stretched-out land ahead. Bright green rice, just transplanted. Barren mountains of reddish shale. Sharp cliffs where it seemed that half the hillside must have collapsed just the night before. And gentle slopes which erosion had split wide open like chain lightning. No trees, no forests, no brooks bordered by bushes and trees, but along the hot road a string of people fantastically burdened with twigs they have carried for ten miles or more. The ancientness of the little shrines set in nooks and crevices. The primitive security of the blank-walled villages. The utter exhaustion of rivers unable to do more than form a trickle in the wide river bed.

It's a land with a turn of mind entirely contemplative. One can complain of the lack of roads, and the difficulties of getting anywhere, but who would want to see eight-lane divided highways here?

These hilltop rhapsodies often ended with a wish that the bike-men would let us walk down mountains as well as up them. One glance at what lay ahead—boulders every which way, single-plank bridges over stony rills, slippery sections where last night's rains had gathered, narrow ridges hardly wide enough for a person's foot and already cluttered up with women and buckets and buffalos—well, it took heroic faith in a small sliver of a man to climb aboard that rear wheel once more, and brace your feet against the small iron spikes protruding from the hub of it.

Several times as we hurtled over rocks and skimmed the thin edge of nothing-at-all, I had to hold on with both hands to my presence of mind. "Let me off!" I wanted to yell, but didn't.

Suppose you were riding piggy-back on a tight-rope walker, and you passed six people with poles and buckets coming the other way—well you wouldn't want to bother your carrier just then. And then, too, there was absolutely no place to get off on to.

The Chinese have a genius for the hairbreadth miss. They can calculate to a millimeter, just how near they can skin by a buffalo and not catch his horns in the handlebars. They know without a quiver of an eyelid, just how far to swerve in order to get themselves, their bike and that cumbersome foreigner on the back wheel, past a baby playing with bean pods in the middle of the busiest street in town. That goes for the buffalo and the baby, too; they never flinch. It's part of the same precision with which they carve their intricate ivory balls, or make the minute stitches of their embroideries.

Certainly, if ever my life depended on getting anywhere, where a miscalculation would be the end—I would trust a Chinese to get me there. They can look death straight in the eyes without a muscle moving.

2

No Grey Hairs

SISTER MAGDALENA is an old China Missioner—old, that is, for a Maryknoller. We can't point to anyone yet who is 56 years in China as was Mother St. Dominic of the Helpers of the Holy Souls, nor to anyone like Sister Berkeley of the White Cornette Sisters of Charity who was a one-man army for good in the Shanghai area for 60 years.

But Sister Magdalena has rolled up 14 years in China and stands in with our ancients there.

At any rate, she is thoroughly China-ized. She wears her collars rather loose and is addicted to shoes with inch-thick sponge rubber soles. ("Such a comfort when you walk twenty miles some place!") But the sign of complete acclimation, the final stage of identification with her people, is the glaze of calm that coats her eye after weary waiting. You realize then that, in spite of being an American, Sister Magdalena really doesn't care if the bus is five hours late or not.

So I was delighted to know that we would go up the river together on a sampan. We would spend a week on the floor, never changing our clothes or taking them off. We would eat Chinese food with chopsticks. Best of all, we would enjoy a youngster's dream of cleanliness; everything south of the chin and north of the wrists is off-limits to soap and water. Living so, I knew I would not only hear and see China, but feel it right down to the marrow of my bones.

13

So we hired a sampan. We had to, because we were bringing up the river a great many cases and boxes. There were crates of old clothes for the poor, sent by friends in America; there was a sewing machine for the Sisters; there were boxes of catechisms and books; some cases of food; a radio for the Fathers, and even a brand new typewriter for one of the priests. All in all, it was a valuable shipment, valuable, that is, for the continuance of our work.

I was useless, of course. Sister Magdalena sat me under the semi-circular mat roofing. "Don't pile any crates on top of her," she instructed the carriers. "In front and behind and all around, but not on top of her."

Floor boards were lifted up (a very simple operation for they are not nailed down in any way), and the shallow hold filled with smaller cases. Bigger things were stored everywhere on the flat barge-like deck until, from my worm's eye view of it all, I felt like Uncle Remus on Wall Street, looking up at the tall buildings and hoping they wouldn't decide to tumble down.

Our "Lord of the Vessel" was like a live nerve wriggling at the end of a forceps. He was everywhere at once, straddling the open holds, leaping from sampan to shore and back to sampan again, shouting, arguing, joking, flinging out his arms and legs like a centipede, in a tremendous effort to get the cargo stowed in the right places.

We had been working since the first crack of dawn. At 9:30, Sister Magdalena stood on the shore and paid off the coolies with wads of money. Poor fellows. You could see it shrink as they stuffed it into their pockets. $10,000 or $20,000 for a few hours work? What of it? By noon, rice would be double what it was last night.

All ready? Good, we were to start at ten.

Ten o'clock came and went. So did eleven. So did twelve and one. We opened a box of crackers. No use cooking when we would be in the hurly-burly of shoving off at any minute. The boatmen came and went; folks in the sampan beside us had a family row; the ceaseless milling of carriers, shoulder poles, baskets, children, animals alive and dead—the whole turmoil of

EASY DOES IT! A STEADY EYE WILL GET YOU ACROSS.

THE BICYCLE-TAXI IN CHINA SAVES MANY A WEARY
MILE BY FOOT.

MONSIGNOR'S JEEP BOUNCES ALONG CHINA'S ROAD AS IN ITS OWN
HABITAT.

Off for a week on a boat where life is blissfully simple.

The prisoners were crowded behind, but we sat up front with the driver.

A NEIGHBORLY CHAT. THESE FAMILIES LIVE ON THE SAMPANS.

ON THE CANTON JUNK, THE SLEEPING SHELVES WERE ALMOST EMPTY.

Top, left, WE GO BY TRUCK IN HAWAII. *Right*, THE CARETELA DOES IN THE PHILIPPINES. *Bottom, left*, THE BICYCLE RIG IN HONG KONG. *Right*, SOMETIMES, ONLY A MULE GETS YOU THERE!

wheelless traffic on a Chinese riverfront changed from minute to minute.

Late in the afternoon, a terrific rumpus came through the riverfront crowds, like a swirling eddy you see coming toward you in a river. It advanced nearer and nearer, came over our plank from the shore, and stopped dead in front of Sister Magdalena and me as we sat calmly on the floor. The storm-center was two boatmen, our Lord of the Vessel, very indignant and the other chap terribly harried. They pointed at us again and again, yelling and gesticulating like maniacs. I prayed furiously.

But Sister Magdalena kept saying, "He, he," quite calmly.

"Look at those two!" shouted the Lord of our Vessel. "You ought to see the big church they've got in Kaying! You should see the good work they do to everybody! You can't treat people like that as if they were nobodies. That sort of person can't sit here all day and sleep here all night waiting for the likes of you to get started. We've got to pull out of here some time today!"

The other fellow, sweating gumdrops though he was, was not to be browbeaten. He was the owner of the motorboat which had been hired to pull our sampan up the river. "I'm telling you," he shouted back, "I've been ready since morning, but the mandarin won't give me a permit until I pay him more squeeze, and I haven't got it. That's that!"

It was all over in a minute. Everybody, good friends again, and my clutch on the rosary relaxed.

Rainy and cold; early April evening. The Lord of the Vessel set his lanky frame on a packing case and got a shave and a haircut; the boatmen rinsed their laundry in the muddy river and strung it on poles under the matshed; the Lord's small son beat his drum to make the baby gurgle; Sister Magdalena sewed on a handkerchief and I propped myself against the side of the boat and typed a few letters on my knees. Altogether, we were one happy family on board, carrying on our little activities as if we were gathered around the lamplight in the old homestead. It mattered little to anyone that our breath came in white steam and rigor mortis had set in on fingers.

So—we stayed there all night, sleeping on the floor, wrapped in blankets, fully dressed, with the everlasting hurly-burly of the riverfront not ten feet away. One arm was flung around the suit-case; the other hugged that new typewriter. I smiled to myself; it must feel like this to sleep on a park bench or in a Bowery doorway.

The moonlight showed boatmen huddled all over the floor. It would have been a long-legged thief who could have navi-gated over that deck. I awoke during the night to feel inter-mittent pressure against my feet; it was the shock-haired, wash-the-deck boy whose regular breathing pushed his ribs against my feet.

We started the next morning.

Sampan life is beautifully simple. Live it for a week or so, and you can see why few Chinese have grey hair.

In the morning, you unroll from the blankets on the floor, dab a bit of cold water around the face, swish not too enthusi-astically with a toothbrush and call it a complete toilet.

You are quite comfy. Your basin, washcloth, comb, etc., rest on a handy beam. Your shoes, for you must not wear them around the boat, stand on a bag of charcoal nearby. Your rice-bowl, china spoon and chopsticks are convenient. The place is home-y; lots of fresh air around, pictures and mirrors hung up under the roofing, paper prayers and bright characters ornamenting every post. Every morning, a boy lights four or five joss sticks and thrusts them here and there around the boat, making a polite bow to the spirits first. You put up a picture of Our Lady as a counter-irritant to this. You even have a jar of strawberry jam to cater to your foreign tastes, when rice and "sung" get monoto-nous.

Yes, indeed, life could be worse, much worse.

We were all quite chummy on board. For the Lord of the Vessel, his wife and small son, existence revolved around the family quilt, spread out on the floor opposite us. One or two or all three of them were under it all the time. The little boy (about six) beat his toy drum; or watched a boatman whittle a new oar; or stood proudly beside his Papa as he handled the great wooden rudder. In the evenings he cuddled next to an old boat-man smoking his pipe in the cool air up on the swooping prow.

The wife was shy of us at first. She wore the heavy silver

bracelets of Ng Fa women, the blue shirt and trousers all working women wear. She was a good woman, not ground down, nor degraded nor abused. She kept her son in order pretty stiffly at times, but once, when the younger fellows put his drum high under the mat roofing and laughed as he jumped in frenzy to reach it, she gave them a good piece of her mind with plenty of pepper on it.

There was a young boy, too, not too bright, who had a daily lesson on how to pole a boat upriver. And a fatherly old fellow who looked after everyone on board, including us and the Lord. He brought us a basin of water every morning and stayed around while we washed, just to smell the soap.

One night, shots rang out from the shore, a signal to watch out for bandits. The Lord of the Vessel leaped up from under the family quilt and raced up front to see what was doing. The old fellow called out to him from his blanket on the floor, "Go back and put your clothes on. You'll catch your death of cold!" The Lord of the Vessel, commander-in-chief of eight bold rivermen, went straight back and put on his long trousers.

I gave the little boy, once, a picture of some cows. He showed them to the old riverman that evening as they cuddled together on the prow, the old man smoking his long, knotty walking stick of a pipe, the child asking questions.

"They're elephants, child," the old fellow said, pointing to the cows. And what's more, he meant it.

We said nothing. What's the use, when neither one would ever see cows or elephants?

But one of the younger boatmen knew a thing or two.

"Elephants? You're crazy! They're the water buffalo they have in America." This was a big surprise; young Chinese do not contradict their elders.

Of course, the question came to us. And here is where Sister Magdalena showed how China-wise she is.

"You have observed well, Honorable Grandfather," she said. "Elephants are not dissimilar. They also have four legs and thin tails. These animals are neither elephants nor water buffalo. We call them 'cows.'" Pretty good; she upheld the old man, gave a neat rebuff to the upstart, and told the truth.

Oh yes, we did a little work on board. Every now and then, we edged too close to the shore, or struck a sand bar, or the current became too strong for the charcoal-burning motorboat to buck. Then, our men rattled out the long 20-foot poles stored up under the mat-roof, and fell to. Standing on the swooping prow, each man in turn thrust the pole deep into water, placed the knobbed end against his shoulder, and bent over with red face and straining neck muscles to thrust every ounce of energy against the current as he walked forward on all fours. Like a line of grotesqueries, a throwback to galley slaves, the panting men advanced toward us, pulled their poles free of the river bed, and returned with dripping pole held high over the sweating line, to begin the round again.

They got tired of it, of course. Several days of sporadic efforts to keep the motorboat going, ended in one more call from the front end of the towing rope. "Hey, start poling. The engine died!"

Then our men cut loose.

"Say, are we pulling you or are you pulling us?"

"If you weren't so skimpy on the charcoal, your engine would go, all right."

"It died of hunger. Feed it!"

It was a really good Chinese fight. Abuse was plentiful. Freely we received and freely gave. As the rope between the boats slackened and the motorboat slid back to us, I felt we should board the vessel with cutlasses and fall to on the enemy.

But the Chinese never get to a shooting war; it's a good fight as long as the adjectives last. This ended traditionally. Our men began poling rather than lose an inch of river gained; and the engine's diet increased. It never stopped again.

It was a mellifluous week in all. Would to Heaven, it had flowed on to a timeless eternity. Planes, ships, subways and trains may hurtle themselves to oblivion for all of me.

In six days and nights, we had covered less than 150 miles. But each mile was a gentle savor on the spirit.

3

Red Rivers

IT WAS the third day out of Swatow going up the river. Three days of eating, sleeping, sitting, typing, reading and general living on the floor had not done a band-box job on our appearance. Even the old faces were none too bright. But sometimes, we learned that afternoon, it helps not to be too up-and-coming.

Two shots rang out from the shore in the middle afternoon. It was the usual signal from Communist customs officials, and our motorboat with its string of sampans swung over to the shore for inspection.

We waited a tense ten minutes. The boat people tucked small packages up under the roof or in holes here and there. Ah Gno Tsi hastily took her earrings off.

Our stuff was too big to hide. We glanced at the cases of clothes and food we were bringing up for the poor and for our Sisters; we cast an apprehensive eye on the radio for Father and the new typewriter; and said a prayer to St. Matthew. He was a customs man himself, you recall, and knows just what to do with them.

First came a ragged little urchin wearing a blue cap of cotton cloth with a red star appliquéd on the front. Then there was a glittering light and the customs man himself stood before us. We soon saw what made him glitter. Every finger he had, including the thumb, bore rings—and such rings! Great red stones, hunks of diamonds, heavy gold. I wondered that he could write.

He pulled a pen from his pocket, took out a sheaf of papers from a natty little briefcase and looked at the two of us sitting there on the floor with our feet straight out.

"Where from?"

"From Swatow."

"I mean, before that."

"From America."

We knew the implications of that. Orientals think any American at all is Rockefeller.

"What have you got there?"

Sister Magdalena gulped a bit.

"Well, there's a case of old clothes there, and a cabinet for food over there, and a sewing machine beyond that, and books in that case. . . ."

He strode around pointing to box after box, looking pretty happy about it all.

Then the boatmen swarmed in on him.

"Don't believe anything she says," they cautioned. "There's nothing worth while on this boat. We know everything she's got and it isn't anything at all."

His Red Eminence hesitated and they played their trump card.

"Look at the two of them," they said. "Just look at them. Do you think if the Catholic Church had anything of value going up this river, they would send two women like those two to bring it up? Ah, no. This shipment is not enough for you to trouble your honorable self about."

The customs official smiled magnanimously, and flipped his glittering hand.

"Pity is commendable when spent on such," he said, and asked for $200 Hong Kong, about $40 gold, an extremely low tax.

As we swung from shore to continue upstream, the Lord of the Vessel gave us the news with his hand over his mouth.

"Out of ten, they took five of another passenger's automobile tires; and three bales of cloth and $400 as well from that man. He got a watch and wristband from somebody else. You were lucky."

That evening, the crew lay around the sampan deck in front and talked about the state of the nation. Pretty bad, pretty bad! A rich passenger joined them; he wore a tailored gray saam and smoked incessantly through a handsome gold cigarette holder. That afternoon, he had gotten off scot-free by merely waving a biggish pile of papers at the official.

"Communists are good," he said. "They, at least, collect only once for the same materials. The Nationalists were after you all the time. These Americans (with a sharp look at us) are in favor of the Nationalists; yet the Communists let them off very easy."

It was good to prove him wrong. At one o'clock that night, again shots rang from the shore and Communists came aboard. Sister and I pretended we were asleep and our good Lord of the Vessel persuaded them to let us slip by. Sleeping through that must have been an added proof of utter incompetence. When a face like ours gets one by, it's plain silly to look smart.

Going up the West River to Wuchow, we met the Communists again. Not personally, this time, for they have a different system on this river. We started out from Canton on a junk, not much on the outside but quite palatial as junks go, inside. White paint and shiny thermos bottles, even mirrors and neon lights, brightened up the passengers' quarters. This was a big room lined with a double-decker shelf on which we all slept, ate, and lived, each in his 2-by-6-foot allotment of space.

We didn't have a great deal of time to enjoy such luxury. Four times in two days, we were herded down into the airless hold to hide. Communists were firing frequently from the shore. The boatmen knew the danger spots and had us all packed in a gelatinous mass of sweating, crouching humanity in plenty of time. We spent two or three hours down there each time, wishing we could be essential boatmen instead of carefully protected passengers. Once, the crack of a machine gun and the boom of cannon sounded from shore. In a flash of a second, a stampede of half-dressed boatmen dived into the hold on top of us. It was like nothing else but a mad scramble of rats into a hole. The marvel is, they didn't get tangled in each others' feet.

But for all our fanning and mopping and immersion in smells, we were not a gloomy group in our Black Hole of Calcutta. A man beside me smiled one stifling night and said in English, "first class passage—all the comforts of home!" He had lived in Hong Kong. One morning we had to run before breakfast. As everyone squatted down, in came a provident fellow carrying bowls of rice and "sung" in his outstretched arms, while he bent over double trying to run in the 3-foot-high room. He looked too funny, squatting and running at the same time; everyone laughed at him. He laughed right back. His family followed with chopsticks and small bowls and they clustered in a group around the food.

"We may have to die," he called out to the hecklers, "but there's no reason why we can't eat first!"

Up in the passengers' space, with all its nice white paint, there was a sort of "common room" between the double tiers of sleeping shelves. It was furnished with a table and benches. The table was well used. The boat crew had their dinner on it; a woman washed her baby in a basin on it; two women ironed the crew's clothes on it; four men played cards and drank wine most of the night on it; between times it served as a seat for anybody at all. I had designs on it for typing because my knees gave way at times, holding the typewriter up, but "while I am coming, another goeth down before me."

We passengers held our town-hall meetings here in this common room. A young fellow from the North, fleeing to his ancestral town with his wife and baby, told us what he knew of Communists when they have once taken a city. He had been in Nanking and had escaped after the Red take-over. He was slightly drunk, his face flushed and his eyes hard. He spoke in Cantonese with a Mandarin accent.

The other passengers sat on the shelf with their legs hanging over, or lifted their heads from their hard little porcelain pillows to listen. The peanut vender set his selling box on the table; the little medicine man, who had been shrilling his wares for hours, perched on a pile of baggage and was still. Even I, who understood not a word, felt constrained to stop typing and watch their faces as, with serious eyes, they listened to one who might know personally what lay ahead for them all.

"The soldiers are all right," he said in effect, "but the men who take charge after the fighting, are not. There is no liberty for anyone. Families are separated. A man is sent north, his wife goes west, the children are lost to both. They never see them."

The whole group of men, like the cracker-barrel legislators of American tradition, set to with right good will to damn the army and the heads of government. "What's the matter with our army?" they growled. "Heaven knows we pay enough taxes. Our leaders are all grafters, every one of them. No wonder nobody helps poor China."

There was a man on this junk, who was fascinated by us. He had a voice of brass. When he wasn't yelling orders to the other boatmen, he was in some corner watching us intently. We could not help but be conscious of him.

One morning, he approached from his lair, and, putting his elbows on the edge of the sleeping shelf, fired the first shot in a voice to wake the dead.

"Last night, when you were down there in the hold and we were fired on by Communists—did you pray to your spirit?"

Everybody on the boat sat up and listened.

"Of course, we prayed," Sister said evenly.

"What about our idols? Don't you pray to them?"

"They are only stone and wood. They can't help anybody. Our God is a spirit; He is all-powerful."

The boatman had dramatic sense; he knew he held the spot just then. He stepped back into the center of the room and wagged his hand in negation.

"You can believe that if you want to, foreign woman, but I know better. During the war, I saw many Catholics praying to Him and yet many of those men were killed."

"I don't doubt it at all for I saw it myself," Sister agreed. "But Catholics do not pray chiefly to save their bodies. They are more interested in their souls. Your body dies, but your soul will live forever. It is a spirit, too; you can't see it or touch it."

"That's a lot of silliness!" said the boatman, turning around to everyone. "It'll be a long time before I'll be interested in praying to somebody I can't see, to save something I can't feel or touch or know."

It was a good exit-line. The passengers laughed as he strode away. It was strange then, when one of them came over to us a little while later. "That man doesn't understand your religion," he said. "But I do. I believe in your God, although I am not a Catholic." It was like Nicodemus coming by night.

He-of-the-Brazen-Voice skulked, watching, all day. A Returned-Chinese, one who had owned restaurants in Chicago and Milwaukee, said, "He hasn't left his eyes off you. He isn't bad at heart, but he likes to hold the floor."

Late in the afternoon, he came over again.

"This morning, Miss, I didn't mean to make fun of you," he apologized, "but it's this way. You're so different from us. Your way of thinking depends on your way of living. I've watched, and you haven't eaten rice all day today. Yet, I can't live if I don't have rice twice a day anyhow. On the other hand, I can't stand cheese. The very smell of it makes me sick. But I've seen you eat that stuff and you really seem to like it."

Sister laughed; he looked so disgusted at the cheese we were eating for supper. "Yes, I like it," she said. "I like rice, too. To tell you the truth, the reason I didn't eat rice today, is that they cook it so abominably on this boat, and they charge too much for it. I'd rather do without."

"You're dead right, Miss," he agreed. "They don't know how to cook anything on this boat. But look here; you came from Canton and you're going back there. What's the reason for travelling on these dangerous rivers? Aren't you afraid of the Communists?"

Before we could answer, the young fellow fleeing from Nanking broke in. "Oh, no. Communists don't hurt this kind of people. Up in the north, they just made them work in the fields, but they got rice for it. They're not bothered much."

This threw the question out into the house. "I thought you said nobody has any liberty under the Communists?" a voice called from the other side of the room. Big Mouth was ready. He threw out his arm dramatically, pointing to me.

"What do people like these want with liberty?" he shouted. "Look at her; she just thinks a while and writes it down, then she thinks some more and writes some more. Nobody like that needs liberty!"

Sister laughed aloud and I joined in a bit uncertainly. The whole atmosphere lightened. ·

"Well, anyway," he conceded, "Americans aren't so quick-tempered as the British. They don't get mad at you."

This brought on American politics and the discussion was lively for a time. Then our friend turned again to Sister.

"Isn't Wallace a Communist?" he fired.

"I don't know anything about politics," Sister said. "That's not my business."

"There you are," he shouted in good humor. "That's just the kind of people they are. All they think about and all they know is God. They pay attention to nothing else. They just keep on trying to do what's right to please their God no matter who's running the country. They've got one-track minds, all on God and nobody else."

He moved across the room to go out on deck. Like an actor, he turned at the doorway for a last word.

"Just the same, if the world were full of people like those two, there wouldn't be any wars or fights or graft. The Communists wouldn't have been able to take over the country."

Yes, it was a nice, chummy junk. We were sorry to hear that on the return trip to Canton a few days later, it ran into a real barrage of Communist fire and two women were killed in the very hold we had sweated out the hours in. It seems, the owner had not paid enough graft to the Communist leaders to insure safe passage on the river.

4

The Daily Headache

IT IS truly a minor miracle that the *Mountain Daily* at Kaying, Kwangtung, China, comes out at all, although it is only a single sheet, tabloid size, covering a city of half a million people. I could not understand all I saw when I visited its printing plant, but then nobody younger in the newspaper business than Ben Franklin could have done so, I think.

The printing plant has five fonts of characters, with at least three thousand characters in each font. Each font has to have a whole room to itself, where the walls are lined with tiny boxes full of type. A minute window, high up, doesn't give any appreciable light so the printers go searching for the character they want with sticks of rolled paper, alight, which makes a glow like a cigarette. The grey ashes falling into the type boxes further complicate the problem of seeing what's what.

The cuts are made of wood, hand-carved. The head printer pointed with pride to the one electro-type he was using that day.

When the page-full of type is made up, the forms are locked by tying string around the edges, very, very tightly. Then it is placed in the press. I asked how old the press was. "Older than I," the publisher said. "Older than my father." One man feeds the papers in, another dabs the roller with ink, two others get ready to take the printed sheets and move them gently up and down to dry. Then two sturdy printers man the handle of the press, and with a "Gung, Ho!" they set to turning out the paper.

The whole process is performed in semi-darkness on a floor two inches thick with a goo of mud, printer's ink and bits of paper. The place is wired for electricity but the local current is so weak, they prefer their little glowing tapers. The wires and light sockets made good supports for spider webs. This is a Chinese way of being kind to God's little creatures.

After printing, the edges of the papers must be cut off tidily: you stack them on a table, place a wooden bar along the place to be cut, hold it down with one foot while you stand on the other, and slice along the edge of the bar with a razor keen scimitar of a knife. It's done very neatly, too.

Reporters write their copy with Chinese brushes in what we would call long-hand. There are no Chinese typewriters in common use; the number of keys required is terrific. These originals of newspaper stories are preserved in the "morgue" in little note-books which stack up to the roof.

Dominating the whole scene is a huge altar containing the ancestor tablets of the Vong family, which owns the plant. My name in Chinese is Vong (Vong Kou Niong in full) so the bright young men—they seem to be combination editors, reporters, copy boys and printers—who took us around, felt that I belonged to the tribe somehow.

Two other presses do smaller work. A really, really old one which even the editor had to admit was past its usefulness stands in honorable retirement in a corner. When a Chinese considers anything too old for work, it's really old.

One cannot help but admire the patience required to put out such a paper. No telegraph, no telephone, no camera-man, no cars to get around in—and yet they cover the town pretty well, the Sisters say.

All in all, the *Mountain Daily News* plant shows what men will do to get the news printed, even if only one person in ten can read. The more power to them!

5

A Jeep and a Jail

.ANY number of enthusiastic missioners have attempted to describe the unique, fantastic, highly unusual, unimaginable Kweilin scenery, with varying results. My own efforts are limited, due to the failure of a large shipment of adjectives ordered direct from Hollywood advertising offices, to arrive before I left Hong Kong. I am thrust upon the bitter necessity of using descriptives worn so smooth that they no longer catch the imagination. Most unfortunate; if ever I wanted brand-new adjectives with punch, dynamism, unforgettable grippingness to them, it is now. This is brand-new scenery to me.

From the air, this part of the world looks like a huge bed of spikes such as Indian fakirs are wont to take their siestas upon. It's a comfy old spike-bed, however, with a few spikes removed here and there to accommodate an elbow or an emaciated hip-bone. The plane, like a fly who was fearful of getting himself impaled on a jagged mountain, mosey-ed over this queer terrain until it could slide neatly to rest on a vacant spot.

One Saturday, Father Toomey drove us in the Prefecture jeep to Laipo, one hundred four kilometers or sixty-five miles from Kweilin. All the way down and all the way back, we were trying to think how to describe these mountains. Only they really aren't mountains—more like the buttes of New Mexico and Arizona, but not red. Perhaps the best way is to say it is like the floor of the Grand Canyon, if you painted the gigantic columns a dark grey, pushed a few sprigs of green into the crevices and placed a graceful little summerhouse with horned roof on any ledge available.

Supposing that God had a spare half-hour or so and amused Himself with modeling clay. He would shape up a lump into a crude animal, and set it aside on the table. Another, He would push into a dog's head with two sharp ears, and lay that aside. After a while the table would be full of funny-looking bumps. Well, that would be Kweilin. Every mountain is an individual; they don't merge and roll into one another. Traveling isn't a matter of hair-pin curves and steep ascents. Rather, one winds around the bases on the table-land with scarcely a rise in the road. Queer, isn't it!

Some of these jagged rock formations are like rabbit's ears; some like cat's ears; a few like alligator's teeth. One was a tall thimble upside down with a neat little house right on the rounded top. Several massed together to look like Cathedral columns. Once, the horizon reminded Father Toomey of the saw-toothed roofs of weaving factories in his native New Bedford, Massachusetts. Another time, they all slanted the same way and Sister Maria called them "windblown mountains." One was a cat on his haunches sitting with ears cocked forward to check on all traffic. Another was an owl shrouded in misty afternoon light.

These are the mountains that Chinese painters draw; *we* think they are either stylized or purely imaginary. I don't know how often I have read in art books that Chinese painters followed tradition so closely that they painted things, not as they really were, but as they had been handed down from generation to generation. Maybe so, but I think the first generation saw the Kweilin mountains.

There is a saying: "Kweilin scenery is the most beautiful under Heaven; but Jongso is lovelier yet." Jongso is between Kweilin and Laipo; we passed right through it. The only difference I could see, was that Jongso was more Kweilin-ish than Kweilin itself.

This house at Kweilin is more as I imagined all our houses in China to be. Right in the city, surrounded on all sides by the

Chinese homes. The Kaying houses, dear knows, are Chinese in architecture and conveniences and neighbors, but for the most part, they are in small villages on the outskirts of some fair-sized town, not in the thick stream of city life.

Here, my window looks down on the back yard next door where a bride is having mother-in-law trouble throughout the day and far into the night. Beyond this home, is a Mohammedan place; the cries to Allah in the morning do right well as an alarm clock. The alleyway before us is so narrow that not even a jeep can squeeze up to our front door; we must leave it at the corner and walk down the crooked alleyway to home, saying a word or two to the woman doing her washing on her front stoop or making a wide detour around some toddler who tries out his brand new accomplishment of walking right down the middle of the lane. There is a public well at the end of our street and carriers go splashing past all day long. As a result, we rejoice in the name of our street, "Never-Gets-Dry Alley." Truer word was never said.

Kweilin's a big city (150,000), but like all Chinese cities, the traffic is almost 100% on foot. Rickshaws, wooden carts, wheelbarrows—these are the only wheeled traffic on the streets except for a very rare bus or truck or the Father's jeep. Yet, policemen on duty at every intersection and traffic islands try hard to make one believe that the evening rush must be like good old Broadway and 42nd Street. When the jeep hurtles near an intersection, Father blows his horn. The policeman goes through tremendous gyrations as if he were stopping a phalanx of trucks, pleasure cars, buses and street cars, and then grandiloquently waves us on. Not a thing has stopped; no coolie with his carrying pole has even looked up; no rickshaw has swerved an inch from his intended path; no one has applauded a beautiful performance. But the traffic policeman has done his duty as taught him in books, and cleared a path for the Catholic Church "en jeep" as it were.

Six of us Sisters were going in a jeep down a through street in Kweilin one morning when a truck came at a fair pace, not too fast, out of a side street. Father stepped on the gas to get by safely. If the truck had slackened in the slightest or swerved a bit, he would have missed. But it came right on. It hit us twice, the second time on the bounce. The first blow was squarely on me; I

I USED THE SIGN-LANGUAGE MOST OF THE TIME AND GOT ALONG
PRETTY WELL WITH EVERYBODY.

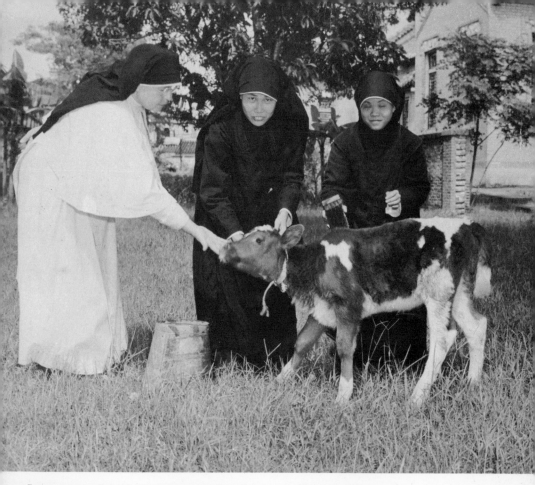

It takes three to feed the convent calf at Kongmoon.

They think my English is funny, but my Chinese is queerer yet.

THE WATER BUFFALO STARES THE CAMERA STRAIGHT IN THE EYE.

"IF WE COME EVERY DAY, WILL YOU TELL US ABOUT GOD?"

To bring the light of Faith—that is our work.

Left, Careful, sonny! You'll trip on your hankie. *Right*, These rich farmers lived in a fortress.

was thrown from the front seat to the pavement under the truck. I don't remember how I got there, but lying flat on my back on the street, I opened my eyes to see the truck body passing over me. "Those back wheels!" I thought, and knew I must roll out of their way as fast as I could. I remember wrenching myself to the left. Then came the danger of the jeep wheels, for I was right between the two; the force of the collision had swung the jeep around until there was only two feet of space between the front jeep wheel and the back truck tire. God be praised, this was enough. I felt the truck wheel knock my veil askew and jam my glasses down my nose; at the same time the jeep wheel brushed my right shoulder and pulled my cape along as the sticky rubber side-wall pushed past me. Then both wheels stopped. I was fearful lest they should start to back up the truck to free it from the jeep, so I scrambled to my feet as quickly as possible, setting my glasses and veil to rights, and calling, "I'm all right, I'm all right!" like an idiot.

It was only then I realized that mine was not the only miraculous escape. The second bump threw Sister Rose Victor out on the other side, and Sister Maria out on top of her. They, too, were not injured, although the force had been so great that the entire canvas side-piece came with them. I think they hung head down out of the jeep for a moment or two before they tumbled out into the street. Neither was hurt. Sister Miriam was sitting very tense and felt a wrench in her back which caused her some difficulty in walking. Sister Cornelia, who was completely oblivious of the impending danger, sat two inches above where the truck hit the second time. Besides the dent in the jeep body, the wooden supports for the canvas were broken completely. Sister found herself sitting on some of the wreckage but had not a hair out of place. Sister Imelda suffered most from the horror of the thing. She saw me leave my place, and saw my head in front of the truck wheel. She turned from this horror to see the other two being thrown out the back. When she saw me standing and walking around the front of the jeep to see what was doing on the other side, she burst into tears of gratitude and wept on my shoulder. In a moment, she was quite calm.

Wasn't it all truly miraculous? We got into the jeep again,

and proceeded to the China National Aviation Corporation office. My hand trembled a little as I filled out the forms, and so did Sister Imelda's. Then we went back to the mission because a passer-by had made off with Father's helmet during the excitement of the accident. Here we left Sister Miriam to rest, and we all made a fervent thanksgiving in the church. Then we went out to the airport and got the plane, even though my habit was rather dirty in spots.

My glasses were not broken, nor were the frames bent. My watch crystal and works were fine and dandy. There was one more scuff on my shoe, but the habit wasn't even torn although there were several dirty places from the tire wheels. Best of all, I felt no nervousness in traffic. I must admit that when the plane began to bump rather badly on the way from Kweilin to Hong Kong, I was apprehensive, but I soon concluded that there was absolutely nothing I could do about it, and quieted down.

This was just another example of God's protection of missioners. I tell the story here that anyone who reads may join us in fervent thanksgiving. I understand that since this, our guardian angels have been promoted to take care of people less hard to handle than Maryknoll Sisters.

"The Model Prison of Kwangsi Province," located at Kweilin, opened its hospitable doors. I had a personally conducted tour by the Teacher of Morals and Right Conduct himself.

He was a charming old man, with wispy white mustache which drooped at the corners of his mouth, and unmistakably Oriental composure of face and hands. Kweilin prison houses four hundred men and about fifteen women under sentences up to fifteen years. More than three hundred fifty have requested instruction in the Catholic Faith. Such a large number cannot be handled all at once; successive groups of eighty-five each are instructed at a time.

The cell blocks of white-washed mud brick are long, narrow, one-story barracks radiating like four spokes of a wheel from the hub, a two-story octagonal building where a man at a desk checks all comings and goings. Above this checkroom is a bright eight-sided hall complete with benches and blackboard. This is the place where Father Daubert and the catechist hold classes.

Even in a model prison, life is none too sweet. I watched Sister Angela Marie at her Friday afternoon dispensary work. Sore eyes, skin diseases, swollen limbs—just plain decrepitude. Never enough rice before, and now still less because they stole some.

We saw the evening rice brought to the cell blocks. Cold, soggy, of poor quality, it would take a mighty appetite to digest it. Great lumps of it sat in wicker baskets without any pretense to cleanliness. Prisoners get two bowlfuls of this a day; nothing else comes from the government.

"These men have done wrong," our guide said; "it is just that they suffer. Besides, nearly everyone here has somebody on the outside who sends him vegetables or meat once in a while. And, too, we permit good prisoners to grow vegetables in the prison yard."

With the exception of the food, it seems to me that the men fare better than they would outside. True, sixteen prisoners are jammed into a tiny cell; they sleep two in a bed, one with his feet to the south, the other with his up north. This is economy; one blanket does for two.

But they would do the same thing at home, probably. At home, pigs and chickens are underfoot all day; the place is black with soot from cooking; the floor littered with papers, bits of food and animal dirt. Here at least, the grounds are nicely kept; roses border the walks and there are several spaces of real lawn (actually, green grass to look at!) here and there. There is more light and air in a cell block than a poor Chinese would get in a million years in his home.

There is also an excuse for the food. The prison depended upon the national government for support. No salaries had been paid in three months. The officials were living on private income; small wonder the prisoners get no "Fixin's" for their soggy rice.

What is more important even than rice to a Chinese, is his good name. There is a double safeguard on that in this model prison. The prisoner is registered under a false name; that is to protect his family. Then, even that false name is not used; he is known only by a number in the prison.

As the Teacher of Morals and Right Living bowed us out, he expressed thanks that we should be interested in his "poor hovel of a model prison."

"Except for the guards at the front entrance," he said, "no one here carries a gun. Once you enter those gates, you are one of our happy family."

A handsome officer in resplendent uniform, strung with metal chains and fancy gadgets, one day stepped into Sister Angela Marie's dispensary at Kweilin.

"Don't you know me?" he asked.

"He looks like one of those prisoners," Sister thought to herself. "But I'd better not say such a thing."

"You come every Friday and give me medicine, and now you don't know me!" he persisted.

"Did I treat you at the prison, then?" Sister took her life in her hands.

"Sure," shouted the elegant gentleman, highly pleased with himself. "I was in for two years and just got out yesterday. Father said I can continue my instructions for baptism by coming to the church every evening."

Evidently, the Teacher of Morals and Right Living had some pretty good graduates!

What was the big thrill in Kweilin? Something I was never conscious of in all the statistics I have pored over. It is, to see Catholicity growing almost as one looks at it, in these missions of South China. Marvelous. Invigorating.

The knowledge that we took over most of these sections from French mission societies makes it hard to realize that they were really virgin soil. The French priest came once a year, usually, and ministered to a handful of Catholics. Heroic, uphill work. Here in Kweilin, sixteen years ago, there were four Catholics and a tiny chapel. One of these was a pencil merchant I talked to. (He likes to think of himself as Number 1 Catholic in point of time.)

"I saw the foreigner walking down the street," he told me through an interpreter. "I said to myself, 'This must be a priest, even though he has no beard.' So I ran out to him, asking 'Are you a priest?' Ah, how happy, when he said he was! I opened a chapel and fixed up a bed for him to sleep in that night."

This was how Monsignor Romaniello came to Kweilin. Today, in that same district, there are thousands of Catholics and eighteen priests to minister to them. May devotions on Sunday night finds the church full; everyone in Kweilin I think, at least, knows that there *is* a Catholic Church. The Sisters are a familiar part of the town's population.

And yet, Kweilin is not at all the most startling example of this surge toward the Church. At Ng Fa in Kaying, there was but one Catholic four years ago, and he had never received his First Communion. He had been baptized forty years before and the priest had never been able to return. And yet today, as you walk through the village, children run up to you and slip their little hands in yours with a shy smile up at the Kou Niong. About four hundred are baptized and many others hope to be. The place has a church, a rectory, a convent and catechetical center. Marvelous. Another strong sprout of the Catholic Church.

6

We Stay

COMMUNISM has taken over China.

The Catholic Church is vigorously opposed to Communism.

And yet, the Chinese are asking to be Catholics in large numbers.

Certainly, if any people know on what side their bread is buttered, the Chinese do. Yet, they are steadily aligning themselves to the seemingly losing side. I don't know any natural explanation for it, but it is so. I have covered 40,000 miles in the Far East. This wave of conversions in China is the most startling fact to me.

An instructor of Catholics-to-be told her class, a group of 18 young women, "You might as well be prepared for it. If you become Catholics, you will all probably lose your heads."

The girls came to the Sister. "Is it as bad as all that?" they asked.

Sister faced the issue. "Well, you know perfectly well that the Church and Communism cannot mix. No one can promise you martyrdom, but there is always the possibility."

Surely, some of these girls won't have the courage to go on, she thought. But they did; all 18 were baptized.

Again, we went on a long hike one day to visit an isolated family. The men here were still pagan, but many of the women had been baptized a few months before. They were very new Catholics.

The head-woman of the family was out for the day, but her husband was very friendly. He sent everyone in the house scurrying to the fields to bring the whole family in to listen to Sister's explanation of Catholic doctrine. He was a very genial fellow, tall and thin; his head was shaved for the summer and he referred again and again to his gleaming scalp.

While the group gathered, he told us the rumors.

"Canton is destroyed, they say. There isn't a building left standing. Everything is levelled."

"Oh, no," I said. "I was there three days ago. The city is pretty well deserted, but it is not levelled."

He was a rich man for those parts. Yet he served us a light luncheon in cracked rice bowls. "We've stored everything away," he explained.

"Are you afraid?" Sister asked.

He laughed a very hearty guffaw. "Afraid clean down to my toes, Sister," he said. "In fact, every morning when I get up, I pull out my nose for ten minutes. I'm hoping I'll look so different nobody will recognize me as the owner of this big farm!"

He knew what we represented. Yet he urged us to come again and again. Every courtesy was shown us; he himself walked to the main road with us to be sure we would not be lost.

Sure, he was afraid to lose his farm. Sure, he feared the Red Army. But the laws of gratitude and friendship could never be touched by mere fear. We knew, if the worst came to the worst, he would be one to rely on for safety.

And so it was everywhere. However, no picture can be entirely white or black; that would resemble the strange unanimity of Soviet councils. I did hear of a group which had requested instruction in the Faith some time before. But when a catechist could be released to teach them, they said, "It would be better to wait until the troubled times are past."

On the other hand, think of Liu Pa.

Four years ago, there was one Catholic in this town. He had been baptized 40 years before and had never received his First Holy Communion, nor heard a word of instruction. Today, a community of 400 Catholics cluster around the church, the tiny convent and the priest's house.

"I used to dread Liu Pa when I went through it," Sister Victoria told me. "It was so pagan, I could feel the Old Boy himself glaring at me from every house."

Now, children run to meet the Sisters, and their mothers straighten from the flooded rice paddies to call, "Tin Gee Bow Yu" (God bless you! the standard greeting among Catholics) as we pass. Neighbors come to the house with small gifts of food. Indeed, when the convent opened two years ago, they were so generous in lending buckets and ladders and tables, that they had to borrow them back for their own family use.

Liu Pa has one of our tiniest convents; two Sisters live here in a house formerly occupied by a witch-doctor. Mud brick walls, small rooms, a ladder up to the low-ceilinged attic where the Sisters sleep—it is a typical Chinese farmer's house. The only touch of comfort is a pair of paper window curtains from an American Five-and-Ten, which one of the Sister's family sent for Christmas. It has a beautiful octagonal window. When I die, I shall ask that my spirit may return to Liu Pa and sit by that window. There I shall feast on hills and green rice fields, and revel in the thought that so many souls nearby are savoring Christ with that first knowledge of Him which is sheer delight.

"Do you find the Catholics getting lukewarm as they realize that Communism is against us?" I asked everywhere.

In answer I was taken to weekday devotions, usually so slimly attended at home, to see crowds of people. Catholics, of course, form a small part of any Chinese city's population, but they are certainly staunch.

In Liu Hsien it was, that I went to visit a very sick man. In fact, he had had a pulse of 40 for several days; Sister Bridget, the nurse at our convent there, was mystified that he had lived so long. The family lives in a sort of loft behind their china shop. All Chinese, you know, are charter members of The Union That Nothing Be Wasted; it pained this family that half of their storeroom (the upper half) had nothing but air in it. They are pained no longer, for the family bed, chair, dresser and trunks are there now. We climbed on a stool, and then a table; from that we stepped high into the loft. The whole family went through these gymnastics every time they entered or left their living quarters.

GIRLS OF ALL NATIONS AT MARYKNOLL CONVENT SCHOOL, HONG KONG.

ALTAR BOYS ARE ALTAR BOYS, THE WORLD AROUND!

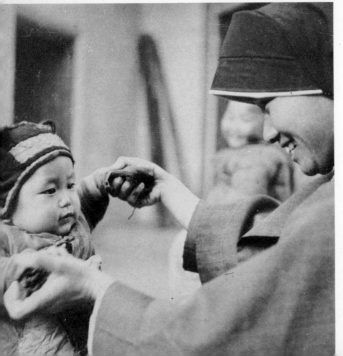

Above, THE CHRISTMAS
TABLEAU IS PERFECT, BUT
ST. JOSEPH WON'T BEHAVE.
Left, UPSEEDAISY! PRECIOUS
LOTUS BLOSSOM COULD HOLD
HER OWN IN ANY BABY
SHOW. *Opposite,* "TIN GEE
BOW YOW, KOU NIONG!"
(GOD BLESS YOU, SISTER!)
EVEN THREE - YEAR - OLDS
KNOW THE CHRISTIAN
GREETING.

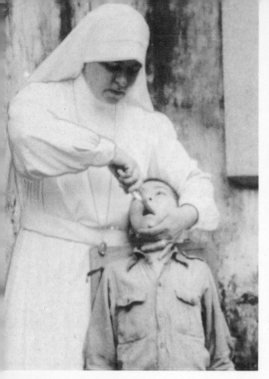

Left, THE SISTER-NURSE CAN'T LOSE HER GRIP ON THINGS. *Right*, SCIENTIFIC METHODS ARE NEW TO CHINA.

GRANNY BRINGS EVERY LAST GRANDCHILD TO SEE THE SISTERS.

"Baptize him, Sister," the wife implored. "He cannot live, I know. I want to see him die a Catholic."

Sister was startled; she had never seen the woman before. The call came presumably from strangers.

"Are you a Catholic?" she asked.

"Oh, Sister, I ought to be. I started to learn the doctrine years ago in my home village, but never went on for Baptism. It was a mistake and I intend to begin again as soon as I can. But baptize him, Sister."

Sister gave a brief instruction in the Faith, and asked the man if he wished to be baptized. He was perfectly conscious but incredibly weak. "Yes," he whispered.

Then I, with trembling hands, made him a child of God.

Yes, the entire family is now studying for Baptism.

And so it goes. In one mission station after another, I heard of recent growth. In MaChien, four hours from Liu Hsien by dusty jeep, there were 12 Catholics in 1938; now there are 1800 in the district. More than 40 girls of the region are training to be Sisters, taught by the Maryknoll Sisters. These young Chinese Sisters are a tremendous help to priests in the diocese. Four of them for instance, supervise the 150 instructors now teaching the Faith to some 2,500 Catholics-to-be in the district. There, the missioner has been absolutely swamped by a mass movement into the Church. Unless a whole village signs up for instruction, he cannot undertake to send a teacher.

At another town, a year ago, there was not a single Catholic. Now a strong little sprout of the Church has poked above ground. One hundred Catholics and growing nicely, thank you.

Yet, any day while they gather around the Sister and her religion chart, these people can hear and see Communist propaganda against the Church. Indeed, rumors are far worse than the actuality. Yet no matter what they hear, no matter what they see, these farmers are not daunted.

That takes bed-rock Faith.

That's the kind of Catholics Chinese are. You are surprised to see your own image—putting a bit in the collection, getting clothes brushed up on Saturday night to look respectable at Sunday Mass, shooing the children off to Sunday School, having difficulties at times wondering why Sister failed their little Ah Lim but passed that stupid Wong child. But loving the Sisters none the less and marvelling that they can stretch pennies so far.

They are real Catholics, pretty well inured to sacrifice for the Faith. After all, when you can walk five miles or more to Mass on an icy morning, and feel that the nip in your toes and ears is good for your soul, you have passed a pretty stiff test of sincerity in your belief.

The Chinese, Japanese, Korean and other Oriental Catholics have a tough assignment. Manchurians and northern Koreans have endured it for several years now. Native Sisters and priests are with them, steady and strong; many Americans and Europeans have stayed on as well, among them our own Maryknollers.

We know what we would do if Communist troops were in America ready to take over Chicago and New York, and we powerless to stop them. We would hold on to our Faith. The priest and his precious power would be hidden and slipped around from house to house; we would protect our nuns; and we would pray like everything that if the crucial test should come, we would have the strength to choose the Faith, relinquishing hold even on life for it.

Well, Catholics are Catholics the world over. In Asia, they are doing just that sort of thing. For them, the wolf is not howling in the desert spaces; nor even clawing at the door. He is snarling on the hearth.

Missioners, too, spoke freely to me. Their plans are made, their prayers are redoubled. They know their people and for the most part they are staying on, trusting their lives to the firm Catholic body they have formed by the grace of God.

7

That's China

THE old Chinese woman ran down the street after us, waving her arms and yelling, "Kou niong, Kou niong!" (Sister, Sister). She brought us back to her dilapidated hut of long-sodden mud bricks. She was talking fast, half delighted to see Sister Rita Marie again, half weeping with her story.

A pot of sweet potatoes steamed over a skimpy fire but she paid no attention to that. Rather, we were dragged through a dark passageway to a hide-out, where a young man slept exhausted on a dark pile of rags in the corner. It was her son and this is his tragi-comic story.

The night before, he had been one of about a hundred soldiers encamped on a nearby hill. At about midnight, they were surprised by a party of Communists, who promptly executed the leader, and subjected the men to a number of speeches. The burden was, "Come, join us. You will have food to eat, clothes on your back and plenty of money to spend."

The soldiers thought it over. They were all farm boys and slow thinking. Finally, one of them rose. "We are honored by your kind invitation to our unworthy selves," he said. "But unfortunately we do not have our parents' permission for this step in our lives. Perhaps you will permit us to return to our homes and see what the older ones have to say."

No Chinese, Communist or otherwise, could resist this appeal to filial piety. They gave the soldiers each two cups of rice and sent them home to ask Mama's permission to be Communists.

"I told him," the woman said, looking with anxious eye at the two potatoes in the pot, "that Catholics can't be Communists. Better he starve with me than fatten on wrong-doing."

There, it seems to me, is China in a nutshell. The love for family is so great, it throws everything else into the shade. Even a political grafter can say, "Not that I love China less, but I love my family more." The whole clan, down to the far-distant cousins, benefit from the spoils. Sometimes the man himself gets little more than one extra wife from it, but grand-nephews and even the left-sided members of the family get an American education.

The foreigner in China is appalled by the lack of coordination to get things done. In thousands of miles of travel in the interior, I can recall only two bridges. One had been built by the contributions of rich men, each of whom had his name and virtues displayed on one of the sections for all to admire. The other was expected to disappear any day, for a very quaint reason. You see, building bridges employs a lot of people; once the bridge is up, these people have to look for other jobs. The sampan owners, too, who have made a living ferrying passengers and goods, are also out of luck. The quickest solution to that sort of difficulty is to blow up the bridge and begin all over again.

Bishop Ford in Kaying told me this story. He had a distinguished visitor from Hong Kong who was to see the mission stations. Most, of course, could not be reached by car, but they started off one morning in a station wagon, the back of which was loaded with lumber.

"What's that wood for?" asked the visitor.

"You will see shortly," replied the Bishop.

True enough, they soon came to a river; the bridge was "out." From ten in the morning until two, the Bishop, his guest and his chauffeur were waist deep in water constructing a bridge of planks. Then they ran the car over it. From two until four, they dismantled the bridge, and stored it again in the back of the station wagon.

"But you were coming back the next day!" I said.

That's just why they took it with them. Otherwise, it would not have been there.

I constructed no bridges in China, but everywhere we went by car, we took two heavy planks in the rear. You see, it's this way. If a farmer has a rice paddy on one side of the road, and another on the other side, he may want the water to flow from this side to that side. It means nothing to him that a public road lies between his paddies.

Everyone knows that rice-growing is the most necessary thing there is. He digs a good wide ditch across the road and nobody gets mad at him. Sometimes in a spirit of fraternal charity he leaves a three-inch board across it to accommodate pedestrians and bicycles. Buses, trucks and other cars bring their own planks. They are essential equipment for anything on four wheels.

I sometimes amuse myself thinking of Stalin's face if he should hear about the Communist officer who let the prisoners go home to ask permission. But that is nothing to what it will look like if he hears of the "essential war materials" I saw in Kweilin.

There were three carloads of them stored on a siding near the city, on the only railroad tracks I saw in China. Gangs of soldiers had loaded them on in Canton. The railroad bridge was out, as usual, at the half-way point; more gangs had loaded them again into cars on the other side. This was all hand work; no such thing as running the car on elevated tracks over a barge and dumping the whole load at once. No, one by one these had been loaded. Then the three carloads were hauled by wood-burning locomotives painfully to Kweilin. What was in those cars? What was worth all that man-labor and expense? Thousands, millions of horseshoes. And not a horse in all of Kweilin! They had stood there for six months when I saw them. They are probably still there. (This reminds me of the mountain of horseshoes which the Japanese Army left behind when Koror, in the Palau Islands, Southwest Pacific, was abandoned. It was a pile at least twenty feet high and fifty feet long. The Navy men there are still wondering where the horses were.)

Again, can you imagine Stalin's face when he knows he is up against something like this? In Kaying, during the war, the

American Army felt that so many flies were deleterious to the civic health. The Army offered to pay for every hundred dead flies turned in. In less than a week, every man, woman and child in Kaying had a fly-farm in a box where he grew flies for the American market. Why should he bother catching wild flies? The purpose of the campaign meant nothing to him. All he could see was a new field opening up to honest enterprise.

And yet, do not censor. No American would bother catching or even growing flies for one or two cents a hundred. Because two cents means nothing to him; time and energy do. But in China, two cents means a few grains of rice, and that's a lot to millions there.

In the Philippines, people are poor; in Japan and Korea and Palau, they are poor. But in China they are destitute.

The scramble to live is terrifying. There are always more carriers tugging at your elbow than there are things to be carried; always more sampans jostling around the big junks than there are passengers to get off; always more rickshaw men yelling for your patronage than there are people going anywhere. Always more mouths to feed than there are bowls of rice. Every minute of time, every resource of the family, down to the tiny strength of the smallest child, must be thrown into the desperate struggle to keep alive. No one may take it easy; even the family nit-wit can be furnished with two baskets and a shoulder pole, to pick up dirt from the streets and bring it home for the farm. Even the smallest hands can bundle up rice-shoots for transplanting.

Cities are perhaps worse off than the country places; in a city one must live on wages. Swatow women are noted for their embroidery work. Exquisite handkerchiefs and table linens sell in New York for five and ten dollars, embroidered only a little. I wish you could see where they are produced.

It's just a collection of mat-sheds; here any number of country people who came to Swatow to make money, are mourning the end of their glorious dreams. Father Silvestre of the Paris Foreign Missions started an embroidery project here at Oukio, in Swatow, to give the women a few extra pennies. Father must sell to the Swatow exporters who pay about one dollar Hong Kong for two days' work—about ten cents a day for every sunlit hour in the day. However, he has provided the women with a clean, light place to work, a vast improvement over their mat-shed homes, with smoke-blackened walls and absolutely no windows at all. He takes the opportunity, too, to slip a little extra food to someone who needs it especially.

A school takes care of several hundred children, free of charge. The children (nearly all boys, for the poor families do not waste time educating a girl) saluted us, yelled the Our Father with tremendous gusto, and finished with the Sign of the Cross in crescendo and double forte, the day we visited there.

Father Silvestre is a young Frenchman with black beard, pink cheeks and merry blue eyes. His laughter and white teeth spread jollity everywhere. He was a pilot in France during the war; he was ordained just before the war and could not then get to China. Just bursting with vim and vigor, he putt-putts everywhere on a motorcycle, patting the children on the head, joking with the men, commiserating with the women, photographing everyone as liberally as any Maryknoller. That's part of his philanthropy; the women need identification pictures before the embroidery companies will accept their work. His idea is to work up an industry which will give these wretched people a decent living and the leisure for prayer and education.

Money in China is a joke. One of those standard jokes which has been good for many years and still retains vigor.

The cheapest cat we could get in Kweilin was six million dollars. Rats came less expensive, but we could not get any trade-in value on them.

Restaurant prices were changed four times a day to keep pace with the rising exchange. A school boy at Ng Fa had covered his books with paper money pasted together. A poor tailor's wife was annoyed by the baby crying in a corner of her shop; she tossed a wad of one hundred dollar bills to the child to amuse himself with.

At Hingning you don't bother with money. You pay for everything with thread because this is a weaving center. You buy thread with rice. Furthermore, you buy rice with thread. If you are outside this rice-thread circle, you do your best to get into it.

Luckily, in some places, the collection at Sunday Masses is taken up in rice. Instead of Junior bringing a coin for the collection, he is armed with a cup of rice as he leaves home for the children's Mass on Sunday.

A youngster we met on the street had a little package of rice under his arm. "I'm going to buy a pencil and notebook this morning with this," he explained.

Small children run the streets with shoe-boxes stuffed with hundred dollar bills. We would send an armored car along, but nobody bothers to steal it. But you don't see much rice or thread running around loose.

Such is China; such are the Chinese. They do things as they have always done them; they hold to their own values. I venture to think that behind the Iron Curtain now, the Chinese essential character has not changed a hair. They still slave for the family unit; they still quietly frustrate any attempt at regimentation or efficiency. They still reverence peace, learning, contemplation, and the Will-To-Do-Right in men, and hold brute force in such contempt that they will not lower themselves to use brute force against it.

PHILIPPINES

8

Shabby Lady

MANILA is an old friend of mine. We've lived through a lot together.

We met in 1938 when the sun played bright on the Luneta, and the twin bridges, Jones Bridge and Santa Cruz, poured their fashionable traffic into Plaza Lawton. You could hire a carromata then for 50 centavos an hour (25¢) and ride like an anachronistic millionaire through old Spanish Intramuros, while the pony clop-clopped on the ancient streets and the cochero rattled his whip handle against the spokes of the wheel as you approached intersections.

Manila was a great lady, then, right proud of her City Hall, her Legislative Building, her grand streets gleaming in the sun. But together we saw the Japanese army roll down Taft Avenue in convoy trucks in January, 1942. Together we learned to make clothes of burlap sacks, to eat our ponies and to burn the carromatas for firewood.

Then the American Army rescued Manila and me, and we were delirious with delight at one moment, and utterly inconsolable the next. Together, we raved over the wonderful soldiers, their kindness, their good food, their care for the wounded; we were stunned by their acres of canned goods, ammunition, cars, medicines, tires, gasoline, clothes, barracks, toothpaste, planes and shoe laces, which were strung for miles and miles on the flat fields where once had stood our buildings. Together, Manila and I poked through the rubble of caved-in bomb shelters for some memento, a buckle, a shoe, a set of false teeth, as proof that those we knew and loved had died here in this particular death-hole, not in some other. We saw and smelled the baskets of rotting human flesh, inextricably mixed with religious habits, the Capuchin brown, the Augustinian white, the Benedictine black, as the derricks and bulldozers tried to be gentle in clearing the mess.

Then we set to work. We were like children, so pleased with everything we did. Marvellous! that the Escolta was cleared of rubble. Wonderful! that the school could open, even if a notice was posted, "Bring your own chair or box, if you don't want to stand all day." Luxury! when there were windows to close in a typhoon.

So you can see, Manila and I know each other. When I left her a few years after the liberation, I thought she looked very well, not too bad at all, at all. "She is rising from the ruins fast," I told her old friends in America.

It wasn't borne in on me until I returned just how far she has yet to rise. It was only after seeing Hong Kong and other Oriental cities which had also lived through the war that I realized just how despoiled Manila was. When everybody you know is desperately poor for many years, you forget that there are rich people in the world. The first shock was Hong Kong, not rich, but all in one piece, at least. San Francisco, St. Louis, Philadelphia, New York, bursting with good things. Panama, Honolulu, Guam and back to my old war-buddy, Manila. Rusted funnels of long-dead ships dot the harbor. A pile of hulks are tied to the breakwater; they have been pulled to one side to clear a path for ships. Pier 7, that Manila used to preen herself on as the greatest pier in the Orient, is patched and pieced together to make it useful. Yes indeed, compared to her Sister-cities, Manila is a pretty shabby lady. The war years are still written stark across her face.

The Filipino loves Our Lady. Even in places where morals grow dim and doctrine is blurred, love for Our Lady shines clear.

"Ang Mahal na Virhen" (the dear Virgin) they say and mean it.

A story is told of a town in the mountains where no priest had been for some years and, seemingly, every semblance of Catholicity had fallen into desuetude. An American came to live there and got on very friendly terms with the tribesmen. He impressed them all with his superior knowledge of the world, his education and friendliness. However, one evening, as a group of tribesmen sat around his nipa hut smoking and talking, he remarked, "You know, the woman you speak of as 'The Dear Virgin' was also the mother of several others besides Jesus Christ. It says so in the Bible." The tribesmen solemnly knocked out their pipes and left in a body. Halfway down the hill, they met a professional "liquidator" (as the Russians call it). "We have a job for you," they said. "Go kill that foreigner who dishonored the Mother of God." And he did; it was a job he had a relish for.

But this was in the hinterlands. Around Manila and the great cities where education is wide-spread, people have a clearer idea of Our Lady's place in God's scheme of redemption. They love her dearly, too. Go into Santa Cruz church in the heart of Manila. Go into it even though you must duck behind fruit sellers' stands and elbow past the crowds streaming in and out of the Escolta nearby. You will never find it empty. Always twenty or thirty people kneel in the blasted nave on the crude post-war benches, and say the rosary.

Like all the rest of us, Our Lady loves to be loved. She comes to those who love her. Small wonder then, that she gave her message for the Orient to a Filipina Carmelite in a completely autonomous Filipino diocese—to Teresita Castillo, 21, in Lipa, Batangas, sixty miles southwest of Manila.

I'm glad I got to know Our Lady of Lipa while she was still poor. In the years to come, someone will give her diamond earrings and a cloak stiff with gold and rubies. A President or Archbishop or Papal Legate will place a million-peso crown on her head. All very good, of course, and right and honorable. But we who saw her under the tin shed, and knelt to her on the choking dust and discouraged grass of the field, will be glad that we did so.

In the olden days, pilgrims trudged on tired feet; our feet

weren't tired, but the rest of us was. We made a regular pilgrimage of this, determined to suffer. Suffer we did, and got great satisfaction out of it.

Buses in the Philippines are built to order for making spiritual profit out of pilgrimages. No springs, wooden benches, no leg room. Your knees are up to your chin, chickens and pigs in baskets are strung on the truck fore and aft, roads in places simply aren't—what more could a pilgrim want?

Sister Miriam Thomas suffered more than I did; being tall and slender in a short-legged land has disadvantages.

Lipa is a place of prayer—you might almost say, of pure contemplation. There is absolutely nothing in the crude shed, the choking dust, the congested road, the hard benches, to attract people who come for any other purpose. The statue of Our Lady is placed in a window of the Carmel, facing out to the people gathered outside. A shed of wooden supports and a corrugated iron roof had been erected to protect Our Lady's pilgrims from the sun. This is all. The people stand under the shed and look at Our Lady. Nothing more. Sister and I stood quite close to the statue but behind about 50 or 60 people between us and the statue. We stood for some five minutes or so, just looking at the lovely face, the delicate hands, as everyone else was doing. Then we said a rosary; then we just looked for ten minutes more. All during this time, the people in front of us had not moved. No one had turned his head; no one had coughed or shifted his position; no one had dug a sandwich out of his pocket and started to eat; no one had moved away. They just looked and looked.

One wants to do nothing else.

However, a constant stream of silent people filed past the window, on an elevated platform, and, as they went by, kissed the glass window pane. The line formed two blocks away, beyond the shed's protection and into the hot sun and dust. We got into it, though, and shuffled forward, and hot, tired and happy, felt it an honor to place a kiss on the glass before her.

I cannot describe the place. Such an atmosphere of humble love for Our Blessed Mother, desire to do what she has asked us to do, sorrow and apprehension for the storm clouds gathering so fast over the world, a welcome to her and gratitude that she has honored her Philippines—all of this makes one feel that a mere factual description of the shed, the dusty, dusty lot in front of it, the approaches lined with "tiendas" selling food or pictures of the statue or Sacred Heart badges, would be inadequate. It is enough to live through these things, and get close to Our Lady, and just look and look at her sweet face and graceful, generous hands.

On the way down from Manila, we went to Teresita's house, where we met her mother and sister, talking to them for some time and taking their picture. (Teresita, by the way, is the young Carmelite postulant who saw Our Lady so often.) It seems she used to take piano lessons from the same teacher that Gilda, the young daughter of our hostess, did. That makes them some sort of cousin, of course, and we were welcomed with open arms at Teresita's house. Mrs. Castillo lives in a sawali house erected on the ruins of the former quite pretentious home which was bombed to the ground during the war. The Castillos are very honorable people; the father was formerly Governor of Batangas Province. But in the Philippines, that means only that you are expected to be much more hospitable and kindly and interested in everyone's problems.

This is the house that Teresita "escaped" from last July 4 in order to enter Carmel. Her mother is now fairly resigned; I asked her if she still minded Teresita's going. "Gusto ko ang kalooban ng Dios," she said with a shrug. (I desire the Will of God.) She showed us several pictures of Teresita as a child, and a picture of the statue with an inscription on the back from Teresita.

Her sister is quite simple and charming. She told us that priests come there frequently to inquire into Teresita's background. "They even want cuttings from plants which Teresita tended here," she said. "But I have to tell them that Teresita was never much of a gardener."

The family took us in to see the old grandmother, now 98 years old. It was she who trained Teresita in piety. The old woman was in a wheelchair; one of her old friends (a marvelous mission picture, with long white hair streaming down her back) sat with her.

The most wonderful thing here, however, was a rose petal Mrs. Castillo showed us. Plainly, in block lettering, most unmistakably, was the word L I P A on one side of the petal. Holding it to the light, you could not help but see the letters. I mean, you could not say, "That is a formation made by the tenuous veining of the petal." No, it is in clear block lettering.

Several petals have been given me and I have given them away. None had any picture on it. But recently, I received one with an imprint of Our Lady of Lipa on it unmistakably. One sees her face and hands, one holding the rosary, the other out-stretched—the curve of her veil, the flex of her knee are very clear.

I even fancy I see a smile on her lips.

"So!" she says, "you consider yourself pretty good in that you rode a bus sixty miles and never a murmur out of you about the dust and heat and chickens and pigs. Some day I'll take you on a donkey-back from Jerusalem to Egypt."

Aren't we moderns soft!

9

Fairies Have Straight Black Hair

HEAVY fingers drummed on the carabao hide stretched over the hollow log—a monotonous rhythm but stirring something deep inside one. Two tribesmen clanged brass gongs with tusks of the wild boar. The bonfire leaped at the chains of paper decorations strung from limb to limb of the great meeting-tree. A pressure lamp of U.S. Army lineage swinging from a twig, was turned up. And slowly the crowd collected to watch the tribal dancing.

It was fiesta at Bukod, deep in the mountains of Northern Luzon, fifty miles of single-file trail from Baguio. All day long, family caravans had been trudging the mountain trails for dogged mile after dogged mile, until the 15 or 20 thatched huts of Bukod's metropolis overflowed with relatives and friends. Even now, from time to time a flaming pine torch was seen slowly approaching down the mountain side and one more expected family group was accounted for. They came in single file—Papa lighting the way with the torch, Mama with her heavy basket on her shoulders, and the children starry with excitement.

The drums suddenly picked up in tempo; the brass gongs rang out with new vigor. This was no time to stand around the big pots of stewing dog meat and talk the valley's gossip. There was a rush to form a ring under the great tree for the dancing was imminent.

I found myself on a bench about 5 inches high beside a

woman in American clothes. She was Mrs. Malinta, wife of the
Provincial Governor. The Governor and chief Road Engineer
were present in seats of honor, real kitchen chairs, with the
Bishop of Baguio and other notables. Our bench was honorable,
too, for everyone else stood up or squatted on his heels.

The mayor of Bukod was an old man, slight in build; his
dark-skinned gentle face and mild eyes contrasted with the great
muscular legs, formed from a lifetime of mountain walking. He
wore a man's coat and shirt, but no trousers. Instead the long
flaps of a G-string hung down to his knees. He stood up now
and entered the ring, standing close to the bamboo cross in the
center. Over his arm hung a long white scarf of toweling. It may
have been 3 or 4 bath towels sewed end to end. He stood for a
moment and let the musicians get into the swing of the rhythm.
These were three men, who walked slowly around the ring in
solemn file. Two banged the brass gongs with the boar's tusks;
the third knocked together two railroad spikes in dull jubilation.
Off to one side, the drummers held their hollow logs on their
knees as they thrummed.

Two or three times they went around, circling the ornamented bamboo cross in the center, and still the old man stood
with his toweling. Then suddenly he flung it around his neck,
like a long thick stole, and took his place before the musicians.
His head was bent forward, his feet lifted high and his right arm
was held high and stiff before him while his wrist and hand
fluttered wildly. With long strides he, too, walked around the
circle.

A woman now stepped in the line wearing a wide cloth
draped over the left shoulder and crossing her breast to be caught
together loosely at the right hip. Her bare feet teetered in tiny
steps; her elbows were tight against her waist while the hands
with open palms were held at ear level; she swayed with easy
grace from side to side and swooped forward like a bird at times.

Dancing was strictly by official invitation. Never more than
one man and one woman preceded the three indefatigable musicians as they paced around the ring like circus horses. When
one dancer tired, he or she surrendered the dancing robe to the
mayor, who presented it to someone else. He offered it to the

smartly-dressed Governor's wife beside me; without a word she kicked off her high-heeled shoes and did her stint of dancing.

Her partner carried a heavy gun on his hip. That, and the wrist watch glinting as he gyrated his hands, marked him as a foreigner. The Igorots consider the Filipinos to be strangers to them—base lowland inhabitants unable to withstand the mountain rigors. Any Igorot can defend himself with a bolo, the long broad-bladed knife which hangs in wooden scabbard against his bare thigh.

There was great fun when the dancing robe was given to the Provincial Chief Engineer. He was a lowlander, too. But he did his best in great good humor. I could see no difference in his dancing, but the tribesmen roared at his feet-lifting and hand-fluttering. They knew he danced with a lowland accent. At last he tossed the stole to the mayor, and, laughing, sat again beside the Bishop. A roar went up in tribute to his good nature.

Interest in the dancing died as the great tropic moon slid up from behind the mountains which rimmed the canyon-like valley. It was time for the great performance of the year. A stage of sorts had been erected and Father's bedspread was the curtain. Bedspreads are a favorite gift in the Philippines. This one bore the word "Recuerdo" (Souvenir) in large red letters in the center. One bulb of dubious wattage burned before this; another glimmered above the stage.

But artificial lighting was merely to show off that the mission really had a portable generator borrowed from Baguio and carried gingerly over the mountain trails. The moon was the chief means of stage illumination. By it, we could see much more than the stage; the excited angels, being dressed by the Sisters on the hillside behind, were plainly visible, too.

Pink and blue angels, whose rumpled crepe-paper wings looked as if they had been slept in, peeped excitedly around the curtain, their black eyes dancing, their dusty brown toes twitching with excitement.

Oh, the whole program was most informal. New numbers were added, old ones taken out, at the drop of a hat. Often, as he came off stage, the announcer was tagged by some performer either avid to display his talents or anxious to be let off. Back came the announcer again, "That's been changed," he would say in Igorot dialect. "We're going to have something else, now." And so we did.

People came and went, stepping through the squatting audience. An old woman beside me pulled at her huge home-made cigar and smiled her toothless joy. We were great friends in the sign language. It's marvellous what you can say with judicious use of eyebrows and hands. Certainly, she got across to me that she attended Mass every morning, that she was baptized five years ago, that the black-haired little muffin with the pink wings and runny nose was her grandchild. Wasn't she a dear?

Behind me, two youngsters had curled up for the night, utterly exhausted with fiesta happiness. They had found my back a pretty good place to lean against and, with only an occasional squirm as they shifted position, were good and quiet, although I sometimes found them nearly pushing me off the low bench.

The program would last all night, it seemed. Primitive peoples really know how to celebrate. But as the moon mounted higher, we Sisters went off to the Mayor's hut where two rooms were saved for the four of us. Some of the family had already bedded down on the floor under a huge mosquito net stretched from the four corners of the main room. We stepped gingerly around it in the dark, in mortal fear of being beheaded by the strings which held it up, and gained the comparative privacy of the rooms given us.

Slowly, I came to consciousness again. The moon was flooding my face with light, and what was that silvery faint sound? Children's voices it seemed and a faint rumble beneath.

I looked out the glassless window. The grassy plaza was empty now, the great meeting-tree stood silent and alone, drenched in moonlight. Alone? No, fairies were dancing beside it. The children were out for a good time, refreshed and lively after their early evening naps. Light, little fingers thrummed on the taut carabao hides; small dainty figures swayed and swooped and teetered on bare feet. And the silver chatter of children rose high in the moonlight. I recognized the two who had been so sodden with sleep leaning up against my back a few hours before, and smiled at them. Laughing delightedly they danced and danced, using the same gestures as their elders, but much more gracefully, much less solemnly.

Every drop of Irish blood in me burbled as I stood breathless by the window. I too, like my ancestors, have seen elves and pixies at their moonlight revels.

The sun shot his first shafts into the valley as we walked down the rocky path between Bukod's houses to the fiesta Mass the next morning. But already everybody was up. The houses were too full of company for anyone to get dressed inside. The Governor was shaving before a mirror hung from a small tree; he smiled broadly and paused for a resounding "Good morning, Sisters!" Others looked up with dripping faces from their basins of water, or unmuffled themselves from a towel to call their greetings. One little girl was halfway through her dress, and struggled violently to get her head out of the neck-hole in time to scream her "Good morning, Seestahs!"

The visitors who had spent the night stretched out under the trees were up, too, and washing for fiesta. Some ingenious engineering mind had constructed an aqueduct, making a trough of curved banana plant stems, to bring the waters of the mountain spring over to these transients' camping place. It worked beautifully. With basins and pails borrowed from friends in Bukod, the great bathing of the year was going on. The "little brown bares" wriggled and squirmed, but Mama had a firm hand. She certainly would not put fiesta clothes over the dirt of many long weeks.

The church was a sight. This mission had been utterly flattened during the war, for Bukod was one of the mountain hideouts of the Japanese army. So far, only what was destined as the priest's house had been rebuilt. It was mostly tin, and far from new, at that. Old 5-gallon petroleum cans cut apart and flattened into strips about a yard long and, a foot wide, were joined together to make a covering over the frame of pine logs cut from the hillside. The roof was second-hand corrugated iron, pieced and patched with Belgian thrift until it was rainproof.

Inside, no partitions had been put in as yet, for the whole

first floor was the village church. But you couldn't call the loft upstairs a "second floor." The roof met the floor on all edges like a well-sealed apple tart. Only in the center could even I, a shorty, stand up. But here had slept the Bishop, the Superior General of the Belgian Fathers, two neighboring pastors and the great tall Father Bernard, parish priest at Bukod.

You couldn't call it "upstairs," either. A notched board sloped from the floor below to a trapdoor in the ceiling.

"Oh, it is best so," Father had explained to us. "You see, on Sundays, I can remove the board and have room for my people downstairs. Stairs would take too much space. See our pine flooring? Brand new! We got this for a fiesta gift for the parish."

Already the downstairs section was filling with people for Mass. Squatting on their haunches, or sitting on their heels, several hundred Igorots heard Mass that morning, a Solemn High Mass to honor Bukod's patron, Our Lady of the Immaculate Conception.

Deacon and sub-deacon had come 25 miles over the mountain trails, from their own parishes. Long rangy Belgians they were, with great black beards and heavy Flemish speech. But how they could roar with good humor as they moved among their people after Sunday Mass! How tenderly I have seen them pick up a blubbering child and look to see just where it hurt. Great missioners, these Belgians; great men of God.

Now they were dressed in worn vestments. With hands joined reverently, they passed and re-passed in the actions of the Mass, before the small white altar. Wild flowers in drinking glasses ornamented the altar; the two candlesticks ordinarily used for low Mass were there, but the four extra candles needed for a High Mass were whittled at the bases to fit into bottles of various sizes.

In this church of wood and tin, distinctions between sanctuary and nave were a bit hazy. I felt sorry for the sub-deacon; time and again he had to step over a baby on the floor who had wandered from his mother in the front row. But his years in the Philippines stood him in good stead. Not a smile punctured his perfect ecclesiastic composure.

The pine flooring Father was so proud of, was strewn with

people—women in their striped tribal dress, old men with coats and G-strings, young fellows gay in US Army left-overs, children with new fiesta dresses, most of them made from parachutes, machine gun covers and camouflage cloth which found their way by dubious means to the remotest villages in the Philippines.

I was lucky; I had a box to sit on. For I was organist at this High Mass. A portable organ of great antiquity spanned my knees. There were several reasons why the Gregorian was a little off. For one thing, the left pedal didn't work, so my right foot was pumping double. For another, not even a pipsqueak could be coaxed from either F# or C#, but B♭ sounded off continuously. Lastly, Father's goat had taken a great fancy to the Missa de Angelis; he had thoroughly digested most of it. Father had been so apologetic about this final jolt to his fiesta plans, but I couldn't see him suffer.

"Never mind, Father," I reassured him. "Never mind. I think I know it by heart. At any rate, I'll scramble through it all right."

A mighty self-confidence! I was counting on St. Cecilia's help and she let me down sadly. But she was a Roman patrician lady with a beautiful bathroom to be martyred in. What does she care about people who wouldn't know a bathtub if they saw one?

Over against the wall, "Bishop Willy" was hearing confessions. His left hand shielded his eyes; his right hand was raised every now and then in blessing and forgiveness. Bishop Willy— the Rt. Rev. Willy Brasseur, Bishop of Baguio—knew them all; he had been pastor at Bukod for years.

On the other side, saying his office with utmost composure was the Superior General of the Belgian Fathers. He had just completed a six-months' visitation of his priests in China, and was in the Philippines to see his men working in these mountain missions. A great tower of a man, he was, with flowing grey beard and above it, the clearest eyes I ever saw. His English was poor and my French was worse. But there was no mistaking his kindness, his keenness and his spiritual strength.

When the Mass was finished, gradually the people drifted off to breakfast. From time to time I lifted my eyes from my office book to see the crowds outside. Someone had a whole wheelbarrow lined with banana leaves and heaped high with rice, steam-

ing hot. The great kawas (shallow iron rice pans) were being
filled with water and rice; men brought loads of logs and placed
them beneath the kawas for fuel; others were butchering a pig,
a carabao and several dogs down by the stream. The paper decorations fluttered in the breeze. It looked like a gay fiesta for
everyone.

Only the priests making their thanksgiving and we Sisters
were in chapel. No, there was someone else. She was a middle-
aged Igorot woman, sitting on the floor near the altar and leaning her work-worn body against the wall. Her feet were broad;
the toe nails cracked and dirty. Bits of mud and grass clung to
them from the long morning hike to Bukod's fiesta Mass. Her eyes
were fastened on the tabernacle in humble love and her lips
moved as a rosary passed, bead by bead, through her rough
fingers.

Looking at her, I wanted more than anything in the world
to stay in Bukod. How happy I would have been to say to her,
"Tell the children to bring what books they have, and we'll start
tomorrow to tell them about God. Your children will have a
Catholic education—your little fairies I saw dancing in the moonlight last night, will have a better chance than they have now, of
dancing forever in God's sunshine in Heaven."

But I couldn't. Bukod is one of those missions we visit two
or three times a year to encourage the people and strengthen
their faith. But with more Sisters . . .

10

Johnny

THIS is the story of Johnny, the Brave One—of Johnny the Strong One, and of Kitma, his bride.

The story of Sister Fidelis, as well.

Johnny got his title the hard way. Many times on the mountain trails of northern Luzon he had stood before Japanese sentries utterly impassive as the searching hands felt through his vegetable basket for the paper he had hidden in the core of a cabbage. Many times his stocky half-clad figure with the stolid legs and muscular toes had covered the distance from Bukod, to Tuba, Tubao, to Asin, bringing packets of quinine from the Sisters on the hill near Baguio to the Americano Captain, bearded to cover his gauntness, hiding with his wretched band of guerrillas who shivered and sweated by turns with malaria, as they lay stretched out on the grass.

Small wonder, then, that after the war Johnny was feted as canyao after canyao was given in the Igorot mountain villages to celebrate the victory of '45. Deep in the wooded mountains, the native drums sent the invitation for miles around. "There is a canyao in Lakad tonight; and tomorrow we dance at Asin." Johnny and the young blades went to them all, resplendent in genuine olive-drab G.I. fatigue suits and jungle boots. Sometimes they brought G.I. friends as well and were just a bit self-conscious about it all. At first, they were content to sit around the clearing

63

watching the dancers as they slowly circled the fire. But the slow clang of the gongs of native copper, mined and beaten as they did in prehistoric ages, and the thrum of heavy fingers on hollow wood, warmed Johnny's blood. Then the wrinkled chieftain came toward him holding out the long white dancing blanket, an invitation to dance next; every bit of Igorot in him surged forward with pride that this honor had come to him.

"And who shall take the woman's robe?" asked Atab, the old man.

There was no sign of preference in Johnny's face as he pointed almost contemptuously to a girl squatting with the other young women across the clearing from him. "That Kitma, there," he said. He threw the white blanket over his shoulders so that the two ends hung down his back and the cowl-effect draped across his chest. Atab was also impassive as he crossed the open place, skirting the fire, and presented the big sheet-like cloth to his daughter, Kitma. It was really a white seersucker bedspread from some foreigner's house in Baguio.

The drums at one side of the clearing mumbled and then swung into a steady rhythm. Johnny stepped forth to lead the dance; behind him, after a space, followed a man dressed only in a ragged felt hat, a flannel shirt of khaki, and a G-string around his loins, the long narrow tails of which flapped between his legs almost to his knees. He carried a copper gong, bonging it in slow time as he walked after Johnny, round and round the fire. Two other musicians followed him, similarly dressed; one struck two iron railroad spikes together in dull jubilation; the other ting-ting-ed on a real orchestral triangle.

The four men merely walked around the fire for several circuits in slow rhythm. Then Kitma joined them, slipping into the space behind Johnny. Johnny started the long strides of the male dancer; his head bent forward and his straight arms as far back as he could reach them. Then one arm came forward above his head and the hand twisted at the wrist; the gesture was repeated with the other arm. That was all there was to Johnny's dance; the visiting American soldiers thought it ridiculously simple, even inane.

But Kitma really danced. She wrapped the cloth around her

and draped the end over one shoulder. She raised her hands, palms up, to shoulder height, and kept them immovable in this position. Teetering on her bare toes over the rough, pebbly ground, she swayed at the waist from side to side. At times she made bird-like swoops forward; at others, the men behind her slowed to let her lag behind Johnny. The grace of her head with its lank, black hair falling first over one shoulder and then over the other as her body bent to right and left, the unsteady light of the fire, the teetering feet and rigid arms and hands—it seemed to the tribesmen sitting on their heels in the great circle, that she was dignity and beauty and art incarnate.

They were tired at last. The jungle boots and unaccustomed clothes were heavy and hot, and Johnny stepped out of the clearing quite abruptly without a backward glance at Kitma. Indeed, he had not so much as recognized her presence behind him at all. Kitma, too, when she had danced around to the group of girls again, quite suddenly slipped off the bedspread, threw it over her father's arm and walked with her ordinary heavy Igorot tread to her place.

But it was after that dance, that both Johnny and Kitma knew what they knew, and knew that both knew it.

That was in May, 1945. It was June when Atab formally gave his daughter in pagan marriage to Johnny at a canyao of such proportions that even Atab, owner of three carabaos though he was, went into debt for it. But Johnny was not quite as happy as he expected to be at the canyao. The very sound of his name disturbed him as it was spoken again and again in toasts when the gourd of tuba, the native coconut wine, passed from old man, to young man, to old women, and around the circle once more.

For Johnny had no Igorot name. Or rather, no one remembered what he was called before his mother had taken him and his brother Joseph to the Maryknoll Convent near Baguio to be baptized. It was Sister Matthew then who had taught the doctrine to his mother, but she left a few years afterwards. Sister Fidelis was his friend, in the early days before the war. Sister Fidelis—her strong face and deep mannish voice, her flash of big white teeth in sudden humor, her sharp cleavage of "Right!" and

"Wrong!," her rapid stride from village to village, teaching, cajoling, correcting, winning by kindness and retaining by righteousness.

But four years of upset and war is a long time to a young man. His mother was dead, now; Joseph went off to the lowlands when the Japanese were after him. Sister Fidelis was taken to the concentration camp in 1942. The Japanese officers occupied the convent on the hill for a while then; and dug deep tunnels and caves to hide themselves from American planes. Now it stood, half-ruined and empty, on the road to Baguio, an abandoned tank in the driveway and a big gun crouching uselessly under the pine trees at the side. Johnny had passed it many times, and always he thought of Sunday mornings when he and his mother and brother walked the long trail for Sunday Mass and catechism lessons afterward.

So Johnny frowned a bit at his wedding canyao, and Kitma pouted at him for it.

"Later, I will straighten this out," he promised himself, and took Kitma to his new house in the rice fields.

It was perhaps two months later that he met Sister Fidelis on the road. Life was beginning to stir again in Baguio after the near-annihilation of carpet bombings. He hoped to sell a few extra cabbages and camotes to folks who had thrown up rusty tin shelters on the ruins of their burned houses.

He was honestly glad to see her although he knew what was coming.

"I hear you are married to Kitma, daughter of Atab, Johnny," Sister Fidelis fired the first shot.

"You have heard right, Sister."

"That was a pagan marriage. Now you will come before the priest for the Sacrament of Matrimony, won't you?"

Johnny looked at his toes for some time.

"Kitma does not like," he said.

Then the judgment came, as he knew it would.

"It is wrong for you to live with her, Johnny, unless you are first married before the priest."

"Kitma is very beautiful, Sister. She is good, too. You know her well."

"It is wrong, Johnny."

"Atab is quite rich. He has given us, recently, a fine carabao."

"Still, it is wrong, Johnny."

"Already, we have good hopes for a child, Sister."

"Provide for the child, Johnny. But it is wrong to live with her until you are married."

And he got no further than that with her. At last, he said:

"You will come to my house, Sister, and talk to Kitma. She says she likes you. Perhaps then, she will consent."

But Sister Fidelis shook her head and flashed her broad smile.

"This is your battle for right, Johnny. Win it for yourself."

In the year that followed, Sister Fidelis heard news of Johnny from time to time. He left Kitma right after the rice harvest—left her with the sacks piled high in the main room, piled high under the house, stuffed into the granary shed alongside. Kitma would not have to work for many months to come. Then he went off to work in the mines away up north.

Sister stopped sometimes in the neat palm-thatched hut as she went around visiting the villages. Kitma was always polite. She offered her dog meat and soup and a bag of sweet potatoes to take home, but there was no disguising her self-confidence.

"Johnny will come to see the baby, Sister. He will come and then, he will stay with me."

Johnny did come when the baby was born; he came, stayed for a few hours, and went off again. Kitma, in anger, went to her father for a tribal divorce.

Seven old men, each a chieftain in his village, sat on their heels in a circle on the clean swept earth underneath Kitma's house. They were chieftains, but wore G.I. shirts and trousers, now quite old, quite dirty, quite ill-fitting. Some few had jungle boots as well, but most would rather grip the ground with their toes in the good old-fashioned way. However, there was no doubt of the infiltration of America among the children; bright plastic hair pins, little dresses and shirts made of army toweling, and the inevitable bubble-gum were everywhere.

But jungle boots, toweling and bubble-gum were immaterial to the business of the moment. The old men were awaiting the appearance of Johnny to present his side of the current divorce case.

Johnny had stopped to see Sister Fidelis on the way. She had gone out to the villages, the other Sisters told him. But he met her on the road, with Acop and Hensa, the Catholics.

"I am not the Strong One, now, Sister," he told her. "I am weak. I will go to meet the elders, but I cannot rely on myself. You must pray."

"We will pray together, Johnny. Take my crucifix with you," she had said. "Then I will go to the village of Atab with you although I cannot take part in the council. You must fight them all yourself."

Sister stayed at Acop's house in the village and prayed. Johnny went on to take his place in the council, opposite Atab. The seven old chieftains shifted a little to make room for him, and he, too, squatted on his heels in silence. Kitma stood behind her father, nursing her baby. Her black eyes slanted resentment and humiliation, but there was deep questioning, too. She knew, she *knew* that he loved her. Every device of bamboo wireless had failed to find another woman in the case. The love which drew him from even her, then, was for a Thing, or perhaps a Person with greater right to him than she had.

There was silence for an unbearable five minutes. Then Atab pulled his pipe from his mouth.

"That Johnny there and my Kitma, they are married by our custom. Yet Johnny lives far away . . ." Atab told the story fairly and evenly. "It is his God who does this," he ended.

The old men twisted their eyes and pipes to look at Johnny.

"That is true," he said simply.

"My Kitma is beautiful?"

"That is true," said Johnny.

"I have given you much with her?"

"That is true," said Johnny.

"You have no other wife?"

Johnny winced; dear God, how could he ever love any other

woman? Stop looking at me, Kitma! He pressed the hard little crucifix into his palm.

"No other," he said.

Atab shrugged his shoulders. Lots of people do queer things to please their gods. He himself had grown his hair for ten years because he had vowed to do so.

"I say, then, let these two be no more man and wife. Each will be free," he suggested to the council.

No one demurred. A nod went round the circle.

"Wait a minute!"

It was Kitma who spoke. The old men frowned quickly and several stood up in surprise. A woman, even a married woman, does not often speak in the tribal council.

Kitma was hot and ashamed. She hardly knew why she had cried out. And now they were all looking at her. Then her thoughts cleared; this Person that Johnny loved so much, loved with a gem-like hardness, she must know too. "I have his warmth," she thought, "but He has his fire. I have his strength, but He makes him a man of steel."

She stepped forward into the circle.

"I will do what my husband says," she murmured with bent head. "I will marry Johnny as his God wants."

Atab and his councillors paused a little. Then they shrugged. Atab laughed at his daughter. "Kitma, first you want; then you don't want; now you want again. That's the woman in you." But he was not mad.

For nearly six weeks, then, Kitma trudged the mountain trails through pine trees, to the Maryknoll Convent near Baguio. Three times a week she and Sister Fidelis pulled the Igorot meaning out of Spanish derivatives. Misa, gracia, santa ecclesia, religio—things for which there was no proper word at all in Igorot. Even Dios was hard to explain, for the Igorot word for god brought to Kitma's mind only the crude lumps of stone set up in the rice fields. The modern Igorot did not quite believe in these as divinities, but there was enough tradition in him to be a bit wary of removing them, or treating them contemptuously.

Then, it happened.

The fog settles thick in the valleys of northern Luzon's mountains, seeping, penetrating into every crevice like a blanket of fire-foam. It settles thick and stays long. If a man is to get a day's work in the rice field done before sun-down, he can't afford to mind a little fog.

Kitma could hardly make out Johnny's figure as he stopped by on his way to the field. She was blinded by the smoke from her household fire, for one thing. But even when she rubbed her sleeve across her eyes and stood away from the smoking pile of faggots on the earthern floor, he seemed a wraith in the white fog which drifted into the crude wooden cabin through the open door. It was only when he folded her in his arms that she felt how living he was.

"When did Sister say?" he asked.

"Just three more lessons, Johnny. We'll be married Saturday week. You'll have your Catholic wife!"

He gave her an extra hug and stood away, looking at her. Suddenly, he reached for the rifle which stood in the corner. It was a heavy, crude affair, one which he had salvaged from alongside a Japanese body as it lay beside the blasted gun a bomber had spotted and wiped out. A good rifle—not equipped with safety catches and a bit rusted on the outside of the barrel, to be sure, but good enough for shooting mountain cats or brandishing at folks who come prowling around your carabao at night.

He smiled his slow Igorot smile as he fiddled with the rifle trigger. And Kitma thought, "How much our baby looks like him!"

"Time to start shooting for the wedding canyao, then! It will be clear up on the mountain tops, soon," he said, and ran out into the fog.

Scarcely a moment later, a shot rang out. Kitma looked out the door and laughed at herself for thinking she could hope to see anything. She turned back to the fire, the pot of rice, the baby, feeling warm and happy. These things within the house, and a good man shooting outside; indeed, the Good God of Sister Fidelis' talks had given her everything.

But by mid-morning, the fog had lifted. Kitma piled sweet potatoes into her woven basket and slung it behind her. A harness of braided leather suspended it from her head, so that she

THE IGOROTS CELEBRATE THE GREAT FEASTS OF THE CHURCH BY A CANYAO, OR DANCING FESTIVAL. IT WAS HERE THAT JOHNNY MET KITMA.

CHRISTIAN SCHOOLS WILL SAVE THE PHILIPPINES FROM COMMUNISM.

IGOROT WOMEN FIND THIS THE EASIEST WAY TO CARRY PRODUCE TO MARKET.

walked with neck outthrust and shoulders stiff, as all tribal women do. But it was the simplest means of carrying loads on the up-hill mountain trails.

"I'll sell these camotes in town and get something pretty for me and the baby," she thought, "something for Saturday week."

Johnny, Jr., was slung around her hip on a comfy hammock of ragged cloth, and Kitma set out on the five-mile hike to Baguio glowing with deep content.

It wasn't far away, that she found Johnny—just where her cabin path met the dirt road. She found him sprawled in the thick mountain fern, with his foot still against the stone which had tripped him, and his face a mass of blood. The bullet had gone through his eye and out the top of his head. The explanation was plain: he had fallen and the rifle went off as he fell.

The Japanese rifle had revenged the nation that made it, and the corpse he stole it from.

"This is the end of things for Kitma," Sister Fidelis said to herself as she watched her pass among the guests at the funeral feast the next day. "She won't be able to stand Atab's reasoning, 'If you had let Johnny and his God alone, you wouldn't have brought this bad luck on yourself.' They'll tell her this shows only one thing, 'The tribal gods have their ways of getting back at Catholics.'"

"I must say," she admitted to herself, "he has a wonderful example to point out here."

But Kitma was at the convent for the next lesson-day. She had very little to say.

"Johnny loved his God. I do, too."

And on Saturday as planned, she and the baby were baptized.

And now begins the pay-off in this story.

Other young tribesmen were not slow in coming to Kitma's door. They brought their fighting cocks and tried to make her admire the glossy feathers and proud combs. They offered to dig her sweet potatoes and plant her rice.

But to their propositions she had only one answer.

"You no Catholic, I no marry." And that was that.

Apo was not so easily put off. He knew a good woman when he saw one, and knew where to put pressure to get her. He went to Atab, her father.

Atab pulled at his pipe as he listened and watched, with a distant eye, his two best pigs rooting in the dusty cabin yard.

"It's woman-foolishness," Apo was saying. "All right for Johnny to tell his wife what god to go after—but no man takes his orders from a woman. You tell Kitma, Atab; you're her father. She'll listen to you. Besides, as chief, you owe it to the tribe to keep to our ancient beliefs.

"It isn't as if I come empty-handed, either, Honorable Chief. You don't need to be told that Kitma could do worse. And Kitma—well, I've got to have her, Atab, that's all. There's nobody else can match her."

The hot, half-choked voice stopped. Yet Atab merely pulled out his pipe stem and rubbed it meditatively through his hair. Then he put it back into his mouth, rose and turned to go inside.

"Well, what do you say, Atab?" Apo pressed forward.

"I say this, young man," and the blurred old eyes looked straight ahead. "Kitma knows her own mind. If you want to marry Kitma, do what Kitma says." With that he went inside.

And Apo did!

11

No Answers in the Book

IN THE history and geography books, you will find the Igorots of Northern Luzon classified as "semi-civilized." And so I suppose they are. They live in grass-thatched huts and few villages have more than a dozen such small huts; many live in isolation away out in the mountains. They till their own rice fields and sweet potato patches; they bring their surplus produce to the Baguio market using their own two feet for transportation and their own salesmanship to get rid of it. Some work in gold mines which are operated by foreign interests, but they stop as soon as they have enough money to last until next week. In such a life, there's plenty of time to sit and think; or, if you prefer, just to sit.

It's not a life to make the world spin around any faster; it doesn't lead to more production, more consumption, more production and still more consumption of toothpaste and movies and underwear and battleships. It doesn't end with a government pension, your last hospital bills paid and your funeral covered by insurance. None the less, a primitive life does offer some social security from the kindliness of neighbors and tribal unity.

And, in the meantime, the only modern problem which really racks the Igorot soul is: How can I keep the children from getting bubble-gum? For, even in these remote fastnesses where news travels by bamboo wireless and the automobile is known only in the rudimentary stages, the bubble-gum of our great American civilization has snaked its insidious way.

The Igorot life is rugged, but not restless; dure but not dour; constricted by poverty, constrained to hard labor, but not complicated by the economic problems which rack the civilized world.

Not so with the rest of the Philippines. Communism here is reaping the fruit of absentee-landlordism, economic imperialism, and foreign grabbiness. The rice haciendas of Central Luzon and the sugar lands of Negros have been hotbeds of Communism ever since the war. It is only the Catholic Church with its steady program for social betterment that is stemming the tide. I saw it in progress in the Visayas. It was Social Justice, but with a strain of Spanish paternalism in it.

There is a hospital on the plantation, set in the middle of waving sugar fields. Cane looks very much like corn, but is taller and more thickly planted. A white silken blossom flaunts at the top of each plant. At the peak of the blooming season, the waving world of sugar cane, bordered by the vivid blue of Guimaras Strait and horizon-ed by a misty purple-blue heap of mountains is a sight to behold from the convent roof.

The problems of production and manufacturing, unscrupulous competition both from other Philippine mills and the Hawaiian sugar industry, education for the disgruntled and ignorant workers, the burden of Philippine tradition which places all responsibility on the land-owner, the rising cost of living whereby a man is not content with a 5-centavo glass of tuba (coconut wine) but now needs 40-centavo cerveza (beer)—these are the problems of mill owners in the Philippines.

I saw Social Justice in the experimental stages. A serious young "sugar baron" took me through his mill and the adjoining model-town-in-the-making, and outlined his hopes and fears for it.

This remarkable young man finds himself and his family enmeshed in a terrific problem. He comes to face it in his Philippine homeland. He spent his childhood and youth in the States and in England. Three years in the European theater of the War brought him to maturity. With this, came the decision to put into practice the social program of the Church.

He lent me a book, *A Testimonial to Grace*, by Avery Dulles, saying, "This Dulles describes the process of his conversion to the Faith, and I myself, although always a Catholic, have undergone a similar experience."

A Philippine family never puts all its eggs into one basket. Even poor men will juggle two or three trades at once. A middle-class family may operate a patch of rice, a movie theater, a shoe factory and a cigar-making business. A wealthy man in Manila finds himself possessed of a gambling palace, an African gold mine, a brewery in Milwaukee and an ice cream plant. So I was not surprised to learn that our young sugar baron's family also had a railroad, a freight ship line, a distillery and a hollow-tile factory.

The task of integrating all these into a profitable business with Social Justice for the workers, is absorbing his every waking thought. "It's scare-ifying to me," he said.

He has ideas of working out in a practical way the doctrine of the Mystical Body of Christ. At the same time, he has a paternalistic strain by which he gives the people what is good for them rather than what they may want at the moment. In a social background such as the Philippines has had for so long, this is the most practical method; when the people see the plan working out, they realize it is the best thing.

I don't mean that the workers are being coerced into being improved. They like the plan very evidently. But it takes leadership to bring them to try anything new. For instance, the houses he has built, all of hollow-tile painted white, are much better to our way to thinking than sawali and nipa huts. They are more durable, fireproof, easier to keep clean and sanitary (cement flooring) and so on. "It takes living in them to make the workers like them," the young man said. "But you can see they take pride in the appearance of these houses, for there are neat flower gardens planted around them."

I felt myself back home in the Pittsburgh steel mill and coal mine district when we paused before a sentry box at the entrance to the mill property to be respectfully saluted by a snappy young Filipino soldier with a business-like rifle strapped on his shoulder.

At the main office, we looked over a chart of the entire mill property and gained some idea of the size. Nearly 1,000 men are employed in all. These, together with their wives, children and permanently-visiting cousins and relatives, make up a community of 8,000 souls. Two hundred and eighty kilometers of narrow-gauge railway runs through the district, connecting the cane fields with the mill. About 100,000 tons of sugar a year are produced when the mill is running full blast. Heavy molasses, besides, pours through a wooden trough to the river where barges wait to carry it to a distillery where it is made into alcohol. It smelled good, but looked awful.

The mill houses are carefully graded, according to one's position in the mill. Homes for "staff members," some eight or ten pleasant but not pretentious homes, are directly across the patio from the church. Homes for the "middle-class workers" (those earning 200 pesos a month and up) have a little less garden space. Finally there are the barrio homes for the ordinary workers. These are paid 75 pesos a month ($37.50) plus housing, medical care and commissary privileges. These have the white hollow-tile homes which stand like sugar cubes on a green table-cloth.

Each house has two bedrooms, a living room, small kitchen and porch. It seems that Father Hogan, the Jesuit who has been campaigning for Social Justice in Manila, would like homes with three bedrooms; one for boys, one for girls and the third for the parents. "We are one room short," our guide explained. But these homes are a vast improvement over the one-room shacks in which everyone eats, sleeps, dresses and bathes in each other's company. The mill also furnishes two bamboo beds to get people away from the habit of sleeping on the floor.

As we walked down the barrio main street, the children swarmed around us. Young women and old, boys and grown men, too, came up to talk. At least 300 raggle-taggles clattered around in wooden shoes everywhere we went. We inspected the digging of a new well; we viewed the proposed site for a school; we walked the railroad ties to where a new barrio is going up—all in the middle of millions of big brown eyes, lanky locks, and shy smiles. If only I had known the Visayan dialect! How wonderful it would have been to be able to say, "Bring your books tomorrow, little ones; and we'll begin to teach you about God."

But there is opposition to overcome. There are "half-educated men" (as the earnest young man called them) who cannot see the desirability nor even the practical value of providing Catholic training for the children. This type of secular-educated Filipino says that the workers would be content with sufficient cafeteria service, entertainments, athletics, orchestras, etc., as if such claptrap can fill any man's soul with content, least of all, an oriental's.

"We must teach them the practical significance of the Mystical Body of Christ of which we are all members," the young man said as we left him. "We must oppose brotherhood-in-Christ to class hate."

So much for the mill. Although only a few years old, this experiment in Social Justice is working out well. Now let us see the reverse of the coin.

The same family also owns a "hacienda," or sugar plantation. Consequently, the next morning we went across the railroad tracks to where workmen were harvesting a field of cane. The foreman let us take pictures of carabao and children and sugar cane to our hearts' content.

The foreman gets a good salary himself. He lives in a nice house in the fenced-off, police-patrolled, green-lawned section of the barrio, not far from House No. 1, the owner's palm-shaded bungalow. Yet he was very earnest about the workers' plight. In a sense, it is the plight of the owners, too.

These hacienda workers (and I mean "workers"!) get only one peso a day, or about $13.00 a month; whereas the lowest employee of the mill gets $37.50 a month. "Even if only he is picking up the papers from the grass, he is getting all that salary," they told me. In addition, mill employees and dependents get free medical care for every ailment, but hacienda wives cannot get even obstetrical hospitalization unless they pay 10 centavos (5¢) a day. There are other restrictions, too.

The houses of both groups were destroyed in the war. But those of mill workers have been replaced with the concrete houses described above. Hacienda workers, however, still live in dilapidated rusty tin and nipa shacks, where four or five families live in utter poverty and confusion. Electricity has been restored to mill homes; the others depend on kerosene lamps which have resulted in several bad burn cases brought to the hospital.

The food situation is tragic. Wages are twice as much as before the war, and the owner is able to get rice for them at reduced prices. Still, doubled wages cannot buy quadrupled rice in sufficient quantity.

As a consequence, Communism would have an open field in the hacienda. The mill people would cheerfully die for the owners; the hacienda people cannot quite share that enthusiasm!

Anyone asks, what's the difficulty? Why be Brother in Christ to one group of your employees, and grind another to the ground? This is the dilemma facing the family which owns both mill and hacienda.

If the hacienda workers were paid more, other planters in the district would complain and sell their sugar cane to other mills. The family hacienda alone does not produce enough to keep the mill in operation.

If there were no mill, 1000 families would be completely out of work and the hacienda workers would not be one whit the better off.

This soil is not especially rich. In Cuba and Hawaii, a cane field needs to be planted but once in 10 or 12 years; cane can be cut every 12 or 14 months. Ten harvests is the rule before the field is burned and plowed anew. Here, on the other hand, only two, or at the most, three harvests can be expected before re-planting. Every two or three years, the field must be burned and plowed under. Women and children do the work of re-planting at $1.50 for 10,000 plants. There isn't much skill to it. Children, four years old, work long hours sticking the spikes into the furrow and covering the end with loose earth. Nevertheless, each re-planting adds to the cost of production. In the fierce competition of the world's sugar market, the Philippine worker pays for the poverty of the soil.

Such is the situation. At 50 cents a day, a man's social vision is not far-seeing. He knows nothing of Hawaii and Cuba; he hears nothing of Congressional debates over tariff. All he knows is that he needs rice and doesn't have it. All he hears is the rumble of his own stomach. As he lies in the shade during the noon-hour, chewing sugar cane in place of the rice his gaunt body craves, he cannot see how the owner is acting like his brother in the Mystical Body.

On the other hand, the mill and hacienda owner at the window of his police-patrolled home, sees all too clearly that if he will be just to the men in the sugar cane shade, he will be deprived of his only means of raising living standards, practicing Social Justice, and bestowing paternal beneficence on his 8,000 mill people.

This is one of those What-Would-YOU-Do? situations. Well, what *would* you do?

It was a relief to get away from this to the schools, where the answers to all problems are tucked away in the back of the book and you can peek if Sister isn't looking.

One of the advantages of getting old is that you can sit quietly in your wheelchair and see what your little part in a great work has accomplished.

We Maryknoll Sisters first came to Malabon, not far from Manila, in 1926. The old Spanish church was half-ruined; remains of the rusted tin ceiling hung in festoons from the pillars; the rain fell through the roof in torrents and bats filled the once majestic nave with their squeaks and smells. The floor was bare earth, pretty well chewed up where the American Army had quartered its horses over by the Blessed Mother's altar in 1898. There were two pews in Malabon's church then. One was for us Sisters and the other wasn't needed. The few old women who still loved Our Lord, preferred to sit on their heels on the dirt floor, rosary in hand and a cigar in mouth to aid pure contemplation.

Like many another Sister, I spent nine years in Malabon, correcting papers, preparing lessons and hoping that at least one blank face would register intelligence before graduation. Then I went away. What a pleasure to come back to Malabon!

A thousand children play in the yard now, where just a handful started. Neatly dressed, fairly healthy, and with initiative, and courtesy and responsibility—why, they're marvellous children! Big boys and girls have organized religion classes for public school children. A new auditorium rises from what used to be our back yard. So many children want to attend our school that we have had to say, "You come in the mornings from 7:30 until 12:00 and you others come in the afternoons from 12:00 to 5:00." A corps of lay teachers, most of them our "old girls," help the seven of us to cover the classes.

But best of all is the thrill of Sunday. Four Masses each Sunday, all packed. The old church still needs repair, but a new ceiling is in, the floor is cemented and tiled, and the bats are getting discouraged. Rows and rows of pews stretch from the sanctuary to the front door. And, like the New York subways, there are always plenty of seats but somebody else is sitting in them.

We cannot credit ourselves with all of this improvement, of course. A hundred factors have entered in—good Filipino pastors, the war with its devastation and multiple bereavements, the example of our good American Army men who filled pew after pew of that church in 1945 and 1946. But still and all, I felt very good inside as I piously read my missal at Mass and managed to take several good long looks across the aisle at 'Gidio.

'Gidio was a holy terror in my day. I took a knife away from him one morning and he sharpened a pencil to a needle point and plunged it into his best enemy. His poor mother came many a day and wept that he played hookey so often. To say truth, I was always a little glad not to see him in the line-up in the morning. She sent him to us, she was careful to explain, only because nobody else would give him desk-room. The mother had no knowledge of her religion and was quite content not to learn. It really wasn't her fault; it was the same old story—too few priests since the Spanish Fathers had left early in the century, and no others had filled their places.

So 'Gidio eventually had to be expelled. That was the beginning of his reform. Sheer contrariness seized him. He became Father's most faithful altar boy; he joined the parish choir; he besought re-admittance and was a shining light in his class.

And now, as I sat in that Malabon church, I could see him marshalling his three boys and two girls into the pew across the aisle. And did those children behave! Not a peep out of them from the Introit to the Last Gospel.

Malabon is our oldest school in the Philippines; generations of Maryknoll Sisters have poured their blood, sweat and tears into it. But, thanks be to God, 24 years have left their mark for the better on that town.

The story is the same with our four other schools—a Teachers' College in Manila, and grade and high schools in Lucena, Baguio and Lipa. Catholic education will do the trick to solve the complicated problems of the sugar mill.

GUAM

12

Sunlight and Coral

THE best travellers in the world come to Guam. It's a challenge to them—like a horse nobody can ride. Guam, with its tricky red tape, its sudden, unpredictable upheavals, usually manages to throw you off any schedule you may have fixed for yourself. Nobody makes good connections on Guam. Nobody.

The force of my own particular bump was greatly softened by the Mercy Sisters. The comradeship of missioners made us great friends the moment I stepped from the 1500-mile flight due East from Manila, into the shimmering white of Guam. They have double-barrelled sunlight there. One feels that it has danced over thousands of miles of vacant ocean to empty every ounce of brilliance possible on that charming chunk of coral alone.

Four Mercy Sisters from Belmont, North Carolina, live out there. Their business is to provide the shifting, amorphous population of Guam with the stabilizing element it lacked—a teaching force of Catholic Sisters. They have seven quonset huts loosely connected, and 33 Guamanian girls who are learning religious life from the first Sisters they have ever seen in all their lives.

Until after the war, there simply weren't any Sisters on Guam, even though most of the 31,000 Guamanians are Catholic and missioners have been there for 300 years. The Cathedral of Guam was a really impressive building—one of those Spanish gems raised by sheer force of Faith with incredible labor. I won-

der if we moderns would think highly enough of anything to
work that hard for it.

The Cathedral is a thing of the Spanish past now. The
American present (after the Japanese not-so-long-ago) has been
able so far only to raise quonsets. They hump and wriggle and
squirm over the island like mole tunnels through a lawn.

Before November, 1946, any girl who wished to become a
Sister had to go a long way for an ideal. Usually, she went to the
Philippines and entered a native novitiate there. I remember
three Guamanians, novices of the Franciscan Missionaries of
Mary, who were interned with us in the Los Banos Internment
Camp in the Philippines in 1944 and 1945.

That was the shorter journey—only 1500 miles of water to be
crossed. The longer one was to the States.

This was the course Sister Inez took. The daughter of an
American Navy officer, a convert to the Faith, she was born on
Guam. Except for tours of duty in Japan and Shanghai, the
family grew up on Guam. Her father eventually received an
"irremovable rectorship" as head of the Post Office there. Soon
after the First World War, he sent his daughters to the Mercy
Sisters at Belmont, North Carolina (his native State) to be
educated.

Sister Inez entered the order immediately after graduation
and was a Sister for twenty years before she returned to Guam
on what has proved to be her life work. In 1932, however, at the
time of taking her Final Vows, she went back for a short visit.
What a flurry in Guam! The first Sister ever to set foot on the
island—or rather, to stay any length of time. She came and
returned on a Navy transport, the guest of an Admiral.

Her twenty years in the States were fruitful. She received an
excellent education and, at the time of her assignment to Guam,
was in charge of Sacred Heart Academy in Belmont. During the
war, she heard nothing from her family except that her father
had been taken a prisoner-of-war to Japan and the others were
still on Guam under Japanese control.

Sister Inez has a real story-telling knack. She drove me from
Army offices, to Navy offices, to the Civic Hall, to the airport,
to almost everywhere (there never were two buildings side by

Right, OUR LADY OF GUAM
REIGNS UNDISPUTED ON HER
"CHARMING CHUNK OF CORAL
IN THE PACIFIC." *Below,*
LANDING ON KOROR IN THE
PALAUS, IT WAS EASY TO
STEP OUT OF THE BLISTER
AND CLIMB DOWN THE
LADDER.

Top, PALAUAN
CHILDREN CROWD
THE BACK STEPS FOR
A RELIGION LESSON.
Center, A KERO-
SENE LAMP ON THE
DICTIONARY LIGHTS
THE EVENING CLASS-
ES. *Below,* "SHAKE
HANDS AND MAKE
UP!" EVEN IN AN
EARTHLY PARADISE,
BOYS SOMETIMES
RAISE RUCTIONS.

side I should go to!). The wind blew her veil back over the seat
and her large brown eyes placidly surveyed the road ahead. But
from her mouth came a stream of recollections that have made
Guam as familiar to me as my own home town. It was in this
way she told me the story of the dead flies.

"During the war, Mama and the girls were required to do
many a strange chore to meet the orders of the Japanese military
lords. Among other things, a clean-up campaign was started and,
like everything the Japanese did, it was run like a kindergarten
contest. Every householder was to turn into the Japanese Military Governor's office, on the 18th of every month, 500 dead
flies."

"Five hundred what?" I asked.

"Five hundred dead flies. Flies! You know, dead ones."

"What did they want dead flies for?"

"How do I know? But those were the orders. I suppose they
wanted to make sure that that many, at least, were dead.

"Anyhow, Mama and the girls got busy catching flies. They
made all my nieces and nephews catch them. But you know
children; by the time the fly is dead, it is so squashed you can't
tell it had ever been a fly. My nieces used to say, 'But Grandma,
there just aren't any more flies in our house.' But she was ada-
mant. 'Well, go collect them in the neighbors' houses then.
They've got plenty and will gladly give you some. Do what you
like, but bring me dead flies.' In that way she was able to make
her payment of flies for several months.

"On the 15th of one month, however, she took out her
envelope full of tiny corpses and counted the horde. Three hundred and fifty. She was quite sure she could get another hundred
and fifty in a few days. And she did. But on the morning of the
18th, when she went to add them to the other three hundred
and fifty . . . Goodness! Those Army men are careless on the
road!" and she swerved out of harm's way.

"Come, come, get on with the story!" I groaned.

"Where was I? Oh, yes, when she went for the old envelope
of dead flies in the cupboard (she should have had a deep freeze
to keep them in!) she found something terrible. The ants had
eaten all the bodies. Nothing but wings were left. Even she was

not up to counting six wings for every fly to prove to the Japanese that she had had 350, really and truly. She called my sisters who were living with her at the time, and the three of them sat around in black despair."

"Over dead flies?" I said. "Pish, tush!"

"You don't know what it meant to them. They had the idea that almost anything might happen."

"Well, what did she do?"

"She put on her nicest dress and her humblest manner and went to see the Military Commander. She told him her story and gave him the hundred and fifty as a sort of down payment. Then, she begged most abjectly for a week's grace to make good her losses. She got a little scolding, of course, but was granted the extension of time.

"Believe me, after that, Mama kept her dead flies safe. She put the envelope in a saucer sitting in the middle of a basin of water, where no ants could reach them. They were the most safe-guarded things in the house."

There was the story, too, of Mr. Johnson's ashes.

"Mr. and Mrs. Johnson were great friends of our family. My dad and Mr. Johnson were taken together to the prison camp in Japan. They made an agreement there in camp, that if either one should die, the other would take his ashes back to Guam. Of course, Mom and Mrs. Johnson didn't know anything about it; they heard nothing for more than three years.

"Finally, the long war was over, Mom heard that Dad was alive, but poor Mrs. Johnson had word of her husband's death. But Dad did a silly thing. He was so happy, so delirious, so out of his mind with joy, that he got on the wrong plane. He landed in the Philippines, not Guam. He was stuck there nine months, trying to move Heaven and earth, which are lots easier to move than some Navy officials, to get back to Guam.

"But—funny thing!—all his clothes and things came on the right plane. Mom went down to welcome him home after the prison years, and was handed a lot of ragged clothes instead!

"In his box of possessions was a tin can, rusted and bent, with the top taped securely round with adhesive. Nancy, my sister, was curious.

" 'What do you suppose is in this can, Mom?' she kept asking. She shook it again and again. 'Sounds awfully light! What can it be?'

" 'Just let it alone, Nancy,' Mom would say. 'Your father will tell us when he gets here—if he ever does.'

"But Nancy opened it. Besides some grey stuff, there was a paper. 'These are the ashes of Louis Johnson, U.S.N., who died in prison camp in Japan,' and the date. Nancy and my mother were stunned.

" 'And to think,' Nancy said, kind of awed, 'I almost shook Mr. Johnson alive again!'

"The next problem was what to do with the can. They didn't know where to put it. They called Mrs. Johnson over and told her. She was puzzled, too.

" 'You keep it for me, Mrs. Underwood,' she begged. 'I don't want to bury it or anything, until your husband comes home and gives me an idea of what Louis wanted.'

"But Mom didn't know what to do with it either. She felt it ought to be put in an honorable place, so they tried it on the living room table for a while. But that was horrible, and they put it in a cupboard. That seemed disrespectful, somehow. Finally, she took it to the priest, and he placed it at the back of the altar until Dad could come home.

"It was nine months, as I said, before Dad could get off the Philippines and come home. And my mother said, as she folded his skinny frame in her arms, 'Wasn't that just like you, Dad, to take the wrong plane! Now what do you want done with Mr. Johnson's ashes?' "

Knowing the Chamorro language, and loving the Guamanian people as she does, Sister Inez is perfect for forming native girls to religious life. She has a natural affinity for young girls, anyway.

In November, 1946, she and two other Mercy Sisters arrived on Guam and set up convent housekeeping in seven rambling quonset huts. Twenty Guamanian girls, straining at the leash to begin religious life, awaited them. The next year, fourteen more joined the army; and so it has continued.

It was a hectic few months, before the Mercy Sisters could convince fond Papas and Mamas that a novice is not to go home for week-ends, nor to be taken joy-riding, nor eat mountainous cakes all by herself. All Guam was desperately curious about the whole project, and Navy photographers did a complete-coverage job on them. Others leaped the picket fence from the road, at dusk while the Sisters were in chapel at prayers, and prowled around the grounds just to see what was going on.

One of the quonsets is a chapel. Three are dormitories; one is a combination community room and work room. The refectory quonset was sitting in the middle of a road-to-be at first; so the Navy put strong chains around it fore and aft, and lifted it by derrick to a spot in the front yard, out of the way. It crumpled a bit in the process, but the Sisters have learned to duck their heads when they walk past the crumples on the inside. It's good for the soul, I suppose, to incline the head now and then.

Living in quonsets has other results, too. For instance, the Sisters find it difficult to keep at right angles with the floor. They are used to sloping to right or left to conform to the shape of their walls. By the time they get into a regular convent with walls that go straight up, they will be incorrigibly arc-shaped.

But the novices are like any other novices. In chapel, they spend long hours looking like angels; out of it, they work like Trojans and laugh themselves silly over everything. Their handsome dark faces flash a smile at the least provocation. They are bubbling over in their enthusiasm for religious life. How eagerly they listen as Sister explains their rule and constitutions; how avid they are for instruction on the Vows they are to take some day!

In the late afternoon, with the heavy work of the day over, they sit in their yard under the only tree that has been coaxed from the white coral soil. They listen as one or the other of the American Sisters reads to them. As they listen, the slender dark fingers are working with shells—pink, yellow, blue, old rose and white—which are fashioned into pretty things, handbags for the tourist trade, and for the soldier laddies to send back home. American women love these souvenirs of a strange land; the Sisters are able to contribute to their support by their sale.

Many times, we went to the poor makeshift Cathedral which has replaced the Spanish gem of the 16th century. It's a patch-work of corrugated iron, bamboo-matting, wooden supports and what is left of the ancient walls.

But here dwells Our Lady of Camelin—Our Lady of the Barn, as she is known in English. And thereby hangs a tale.

According to what Sister Inez tells me, a poor fisherman was out with a hand-net one day, scooping up fish in shallow water. He saw this wooden statue, about 2 feet high, fully dressed in the Spanish manner, floating on the waves. What amazed him was that it stood upright and advanced with dignity from wave to wave.

It had been coming in his direction, but when he went after it, the statue edged away. Then he realized that in his half-naked condition, he was in no state to touch a statue of Our Lady. So he returned to the beach, put on his shirt and again waded out to where Our Lady bobbed gracefully on the waves.

This time, she was only too glad to be carried by the fisher-man. She came graciously into his hands. In triumph, the man lifted her high and turned to the shore. What was his amazement as he came to knee-high water, to see two huge crabs emerge from the sea before him. And each of them carried a lighted candle!

By this time, others too had seen the little lady floating up-right in the sea. The shore was alive with people. They made a pathway for the strange acolytes with their lighted candles and fell in behind them in procession. The fisherman and Our Lady came last. The crabs slowly crawled over the sandy shore. They slid through the coarse grass and on to the ground. At last they stopped in front of the barn belonging to the poor fisher-man who now carried Our Lady.

On the site of this barn the great Cathedral of Agana was built and the statue was enshrined over the high altar. To her protection, the Guamanians credit freedom from typhoons. This is how they prove it.

When Bishop Baumgartner looked over his diocese of Guam after the war, his first thought was to rehabilitate Our Lady of

Camelin who had lost much of her original beauty, and whose clothes were in rags.

Against the pleas of the people, he sent the statue to Manila to be done over—the face and hands painted, the hair washed and curled, the clothes re-made. She had hardly left, when the worst typhoon in Guam's history broke over the island. In a hurry, the Bishop sent for her and placed her again in honor over the high altar.

Omnia Guamia divisa est in tres partes. The Army has the north; the Navy takes the middle, and the Marines the southeast. Guamanians can take what's left. When you have 70,000 Americans (who like elbow room, especially when it's free) on an island 30 by 8 miles, there isn't much room left for the original inhabitants. The southwest, rocky, rugged and uncultivated, has been allotted them. There are about 30,000 Guamanians and 20,000 Filipinos.

Most of the Filipinos are transients, brought by the Luzon Stevedoring Company to build roads and such over the island. They live in large camps, Camp Quezon, Camp Roxas, etc., which fly the Philippine flag; they are practically extraterritorial parts of the island. Huge vans, heavily barred and seemingly armor-plated, carry the laborers to and from work. They seem to be little less than travelling jails.

13

A Seat in the Blister

SISTER INEZ is related to half the people on Guam and is the best friend of everyone else. A strange mania afflicts all Guamanians so that, as soon as they see her, they start reaching for things and pressing them into her hand. Sister Inez has the same affliction in another form. She reaches for things and presses them into suitcases to be taken off by itinerant missioners such as I.

In my two weeks as her guest on Guam, she put into my disreputable old suitcase—cream cheese, book ends, Philippine table mats, cookies, candy, a wall ornament, several books, a glass pitcher and four goblets and a bottle of medicine. It got so heavy, I never trusted the handle, but grasped it firmly around the middle as best I could to tote it from place to place. Indeed, reliable sources indicate that when the suitcase was lifted into the air at last, the entire island of Guam rose two inches from the sea.

I was glad it did. It was revenge in some small way for the humiliating way I had to get into that plane.

Only one plane a week serves the thousands of tiny islands scattered in the Trust Territories of the United States. Army and Navy officials did their best to get me passage on it, but they have great difficulties in getting around themselves. The Palau Islands are serviced by two boat trips a month, but captains do not want to take women passengers, because Navy laws

ordain that a doctor must be aboard. Even if, by chance, a
doctor is going along, then a woman passenger means that four
or five men must be turned out of their bunks to ensure a private
cabin for the woman.

I didn't know it, but the plane leaves every Monday morning. I started the rounds of Navy offices asking for passage just
about an hour after the weekly plane had left.

On the fourth or fifth visit to headquarters, everything was
arranged. I had told my life history, my references had been dug
out of the files, the Sisters on Palau had been notified of my
coming and said they really had no great objections. Purpose,
length of stay, citizenship, activities during the war and other
matters were settled. It remained only to get the last bunch of
papers signed and I would have the privilege of paying $.13 a
mile to the government for my passage.

We were chatting chummily at the Commander's desk. He
had spent several years on duty at Koror, in the Palau Islands,
and could tell me much of the place. Then, of a sudden, he
hesitated.

"One last thing, Sister, I should tell you," he said. "We
usually require that women passengers on these planes wear
slacks. In your case . . ."

"Oh, I can manage very well, Commander," I hurried to fill
the gap. "I promise you, I won't be any trouble, really, I won't."

He laughed good naturedly, and, I thought, forgot all about
it.

Bright and sunny, the blessed Monday dawned, fruit of
more than two weeks of trudging from office to office. Sister Inez
and Sister Louise, her assistant, drove me and my prodigious
suitcase to the airport. A couple of cartons contained the over-
flow of her generosity to our Sisters in the Palau Islands.

It was a tiny plane, which swooped away to nothing in the
back. Two big blisters of plastic swelled from the sides—lookouts
for gunners and photographers. Perhaps eight men could be
crowded into the windowless, airless, black space between the
wings, a sort of tank outfitted with bucket seats, with a door
like a safe-deposit vault. Seven hours in such a place and you
wonder why you didn't elect to swim.

The men loaded the baggage into the plane, lifting it high into one of the blisters, thrown open. Then they put down a short steel ladder from the blister and one by one they climbed up to take their places in that doleful tank. "Oh, that ladder won't be hard to negotiate," I thought confidently.

From the corner of my eye, I saw a "finger lift" approaching across the field.

"Just like them," I thought, "to come along when all the baggage is in!"

The big derrick-like thing lumbered over to the plane and jockeyed into position. Someone put a wooden platform across the steel prongs. Then an officer approached our little group. "We're ready for you, Sister," he said.

It was no use protesting that I could easily climb the ladder. Up on the finger lift I rose, feeling like a sack of potatoes being stuffed into the hold!

Once inside, a nice tow-headed Navy youngster trussed me in a Mae West life jacket, strung fore and aft with all sorts of gadgets. He sat me down decisively in a nearby chair and buckled securely the three-inch landing belt.

There was little to do while the rest of the "blister" passengers came on and stumbled past my feet (curled up out of the way though they were). I fell to examining the junk pinned, tied and sewed on the Mae West which occupied all of my chest and most of my lap as well. I found a police whistle, a flashlight, a packet of shark-chasing chemical, some distress-signal smoke (one for day, another for night) a sharp little knife for cutting off the legs of entangling octopi, and lastly, an envelope of ocean-marking dye, to show just where the rescue crew should throw the memorial wreath.

Raising my eyes from this gruesome business, I perused a typewritten sheet on the wall beside me. "Method of ditching plane, . . . if fire is in fuselage, . . . if wing falls off, . . . if engines go dead, . . . if fire attacks fuel line, . . . explosions during flight." I began to think seriously of all the mean things I did in my childhood and what a worry I have been to my superiors ever since.

As the plane soared along in high altitude, a kindly Navy

officer wrapped me and my life-jacket, shark chaser, smoke sig-
nals, etc., etc., in a big blanket and folded it tight around me.
Now there was simply no lap left; I was one big curve from
my chin to my feet. Everyone else in the blister was all wrapped
up too and almost asleep.

I was just lapsing cozily into the Fifth Joyful Mystery, when
something touched my knee and stayed there. It was a tray, a
smallish tray but heaped high with a great big steak (a tremendous steak!) a mountain of scrambled eggs, two great slices
of bread and butter, fruit juice and crushed pineapple. The tow-
headed youngster was pushing it at my outer wrappings, and I,
like a silkworm in a cocoon, didn't know what it was all about.

Nobody else in the blister had anything being poked at
him, so I thought I was to take what I wanted and pass the
rest around. But the other three Great Curves shook their heads
above the blankets—it was too noisy to talk.

I wriggled my hands loose gently, lest everything go smash
on that precarious lap, and began slowly to butter some bread
and convey it carefully over the accumulation of safety devices
on my chest. It was really quite a feat. Some months later, in
China, I rang the bell on eating skill, when I daintily did away
with a half-fried egg, swimming in grease, by the use of chopsticks only. Furthermore, the egg had to be carried from a low
table at knee height, across a white habit (which no napkin
protected) while a sprightly conversation went on. All the saints
in heaven were with me that day. At least, I asked them all to
come and help. But some of the credit must go to diligent practice with a juicy steak and a mountain of scrambled eggs as I
rode in the blister that morning.

The world of sea and sky is yours from the blister. In war-
time, the photographer and the gunner sit here. Perhaps only
from the small end of a parachute, can you get a real-er feeling
of being suspended in sheer space. The world of water is yours,
too. As the amphibious plane smacked the waves, landing at
Yap three and a half hours later, the water poured over our
blister in a blue torrent. Instinctively, one ducked, to get out
from under.

A Navy launch came out to us for mail and a single passenger at Yap. A strange native sailboat scudded across our path, just in front of the propellers. Now I wished we had Maryknoll Sisters on Yap, so that I might stop here and see this island with the queer name. But, in five minutes, we took off for Koror, chief of the Palau Islands, two hours away.

Rain and clouds forced us to circle Koror many times and even to go down to Pelelieu, 40 miles away. But at last we slipped close to the blue-green water, bumped the spanking waves several times, settled comfortably in the water and set about getting to land. We taxied for some distance in water with our fins at the wing-tips acting as outriggers to steady us. Then I felt a commotion beneath the flooring. At first I thought we must be scraping across a rock, but no—we let down our wheels and waddled up a concrete ramp on to a wide dock swarming with jeeps and bedraggled, rained-on people.

There was no finger-lift on Palau to crush my pride. A woman passenger attired in slacks quivered and wriggled, gasped and clutched as she slowly went down the little ladder. There was joy in my wicked heart as I swung gaily out the open blister, negotiated that ladder with the greatest of ease and leaped to the ground like an old circus hand. Agility doesn't always come wrapped in slacks!

"Our three" were there with Father McManus and the mission jeep. They were wrapped in hooded raincapes but the Maryknoll smile beamed at high voltage. But the smile-voltage affected not the mission jeep. The starter was off, and although helpful Navy men pushed and shoved us all over the dock and for some distance along the road, so that we must have looked like a rubber toy worried and chased and thrown around by puppies, still the engine refused to come alive. So we borrowed the Police jeep, transferred ourselves and that tremendous suitcase into it, and in style drove away to Maryknoll-on-Palau with Sister Loretta Marie at the wheel.

PALAU

14

Bats and Bright
Blue Paint

TAKE a ruler, some day, and measure off on the map an area of pretty, blue water just east of the Philippines. Make it two thousand miles long and one thousand miles wide. That is two million square miles. And in all that space, there are only four Catholic Sisters—four from Maryknoll.

"But we have neighboring convents," says Sister Loretta Marie. (She is from Brooklyn, with five thousand Sisters in one thousand square miles.) "There are the American Mercy Sisters on Guam, eight hundred miles north; and Spanish Sisters on Truk, fifteen hundred miles east; and New Guinea is only six hundred miles south. There must be many Sisters on Mindanao, one of the Philippines, just six hundred miles west."

It's nice to have neighbors so chummy, isn't it?

But figures like that are common in the Southwest Pacific. Five hundred miles between parishes is just nothing. What is worse, this Caroline-Marshall Islands Vicariate must be covered by courtesy of the U.S. Navy. Father Vincent Kennelly, S.J., Vicar Apostolic, needs the wings of an angel or the patience of a saint. Preferably, both. The Navy does what it can, but planes are scarce and the Navy has its own fish to fry, too.

"What this vicariate needs," in the consensus of opinion, "is a giant bulldozer to push it all together. Then we could really do things."

Koror is the center of the Palau parish, covering ten inhabited islands strung out over five hundred miles. All together, there are but six thousand people in the whole district, of whom two thousand are Catholic. (Thirteen hundred are Protestant and the rest, simple pagans.) But what a task to care for those two thousand. Babelthuap is the largest island, twenty-two by ten miles; some thirty villages are scattered on the coast. No road connects the villages; no paths cross the interior. There is no possibility of taking a jeep and riding around to cover several each day. Small native boats loop the towns loosely together, and they run on schedules not known even to God. A mission journey to Babelthuap villages takes the best part of a month, to bring Mass and the Sacraments to approximately one thousand Catholics in the thirty-five-hundred population.

Koror is insignificant in size—only six miles long and one-half mile wide. It lies in a semi-circle, like half a doughnut thrown into the sea. But that doughnut had power in its day. Its two arms embrace a harbor so deep, so secluded and so capacious that three hundred Japanese ships could rest secure in it. Koror, the Navy men say, could never have been captured. The Marines took Pelelieu, forty miles south, in 1944 but Koror was occupied only after the surrender in 1945. Its twenty thousand Japanese were sent back to Japan; today, about fifty American Navy men with perhaps thirty to forty dependents hold the district with eight missioners and one thousand Palauans.

It would be appropriate here to speak of Koror as a "Ghost Town." But not even the ghosts remain. As you drive along the road which crowns the semi-circular ridge, you think of yourself as penetrating a jungle; an occasional clearing by the roadside holds a quonset hut, the mission church or some native house. But for the rest, Tangin-tangin (known as false koa in Hawaii), tall grass, giant elephant ears, creep greedily to the road's edge eager to swallow it up before the next jeep hurtles by. It is only when you take the trouble to walk slowly with your eyes open, that you can reconstruct the sizable city the Japanese built in their twenty-five years of occupancy. Iron disks with Japanese characters show where gas and water mains once lay under the main street, which is now the jungle road described above. A few feet off the roadside you often see the rusted chassis of a truck or private car, rapidly disappearing under lush vegetation. Some of the younger faces have Japanese eyes and straight hair; roadside signs are scribbled in Katakana characters. Four or five concrete steps, the concrete flooring of a house, or, more rarely, a nice little fish-pond which must have graced someone's front lawn point to a time when Japanese Navy families had secure homes here. Wishing to leave absolutely nothing, the Japanese set about undoing their civilization with characteristic thoroughness. American bulldozers completed the job.

However, fortunately, you can glimpse old Japan still on "Topside." This is the highest point on the island, a lovely mountainside overlooking that deep, capacious harbor, dotted with tiny, green islands. Here was the main temple, approached by wide steps now grass-grown, and guarded by stone lions with curly hair. Three tori span the road approaching it and stone lanterns light the way. The temple itself has been destroyed, and in its place is a white frame building surmounted by a cross. It was built as a Catholic Church but numbers did not warrant a resident chaplain, especially with Catholic and Protestant missionaries on the island as well. The building is now used as a general recreation hall for Navy personnel. But it must give any Christian a thrill that, where once a pagan temple regarded through half-closed eyes the mighty naval power of its gods, now the cross gleams triumphant on the mountainside.

So much for what was. Now for the mission itself.

The Sisters have "regular classes," Kindergarten and First Grade. They are scheduled from 7:30 until 11:00 in the morning, but nobody watches the clock.

One large central room on the first floor is Sister Loretta Marie's kindergarten where thirty-four little brown angels with shining black curls and eyes like saucers are perched on benches on either side of the long tables. In English and in Palauan, Sister puts them through the one-two-threes.

In another room behind, another Sister has twenty-six first graders, twelve on each side of the table and two parked on a packing case. There was room for one more on the packing case, so a twenty-seventh was accepted.

In the afternoon three times a week there are catechism and English classes for larger boys and girls who attend the public school, and the beginnings of a boys' choir on Tuesdays and Thursdays.

Three nights a week, catechism classes for women and girls. These are the most picturesque classes of all, for each of the Sisters goes downstairs with a kerosene lamp and becomes the center of a chattering, lively group. Sister Camillus has about twenty women worthy of any mission picture. Caterina and Natalia own in common a pair of glasses with one cracked lens; they pass the glasses from one to another whenever Sister calls on them. Maria is tattooed from the elbow to the knuckles in an intricate blue design; she wears her glasses halfway down her nose, and oh, how she does study. She knows most of the answers, for she spent four years with the German Sisters when they were here thirty years ago. "Sisters were from 'Mee Lwoh Kee,'" she said several times. I smiled politely, knowing that I had never heard of the place, but there probably was some island around there named Mee Lwoh Kee. "Mee Lwoh Kee in America," she insisted. And light dawned. German-speaking Sisters from Milwaukee. These are the women who brought us a magnificent Palau dinner one Sunday—a crab with a pincer spread of sixteen inches, taro boiled, fried, candied and baked, tapioca wrapped in banana leaves and boiled (like suman in the Philippines), and coconut in all disguises. The staple food on Palau is tapioca. They boil it, they fry it, they mash it. They cut it in slices and strips; they roll it into balls. They serve it on banana leaves or in lacquered Japanese dishes, with coconut milk or brown sugar. But it's all the same old tapioca, heavy and goo-ey, a lump of wall-paper paste in your tummy.

One evening, we watched the giant bats wheel overhead. I thought them large crows at first, until they dipped in flight as bats do and then I heard them squeak. These are the large Australian fruit bats which are also on Guam. The natives eat them. Often at night, you can hear their leathery wings flapping outside your window like sails in a slack wind.

Other giants are the snails. Six inches long—and they overrun the place. The story is that the Japanese introduced them because they like to eat snails and figured the bigger they were, the better. But they found them poisonous to eat and ruinous to the crops. Every morning, there are hundreds of them crawling up the steps, galloping over the grass, breakfasting on every green thing they see. There is nothing retiring about these snails; they will use the shell as a last resort but much prefer to fight out in the fresh air. Sister Loretta Marie who has hopes for a garden, loses her good disposition for the day even before Mass. As we walked in silence down the road to church at 5:30 in the morning, she picked up every snail she saw and whammed it against some convenient stone to break the shell.

Last Christmas-time, the Sisters went to a rehearsal for the Christmas program and found a ten foot snake coiled on the rafters of the quonset that serves as parish hall. But snakes are rare, the people say.

Banana trees, bamboo and other plants seem extremely tall. I saw a clump of torch ginger twelve feet high. This is due perhaps to the almost continual rainfall.

"We came in the middle of the rainy season last September," Sister Loretta Marie told me, "and we are still waiting for the dry season to happen."

Certainly, my visit on Koror was the wettest two weeks I ever went through.

Everything in the convent, practically, is blue—the ceiling, doors, window frames, and walls in cells, chapel, kitchen, everywhere. You see, on Koror the Navy stores control one's life. If the Navy Commissary has oranges, everyone eats oranges; if it has corned beef, everyone has corned beef. Well, when the mission had enough money to invest in paint, the Navy offered three shades, apple green, sky blue or white. Take your choice. So Brother John (he's a Basque Jesuit Brother with seventeen years in Japan) chose apple green for everything downstairs, sky blue for the upstairs, and saved the white for church. He must have had a lot of blue, for it's really like a religious habit among buildings on Koror. You know it's a Catholic building if it's "plenty blue." Francisco the catechist's house is blue inside and out, the parish hall is blue, a quonset where a leading Christian lives is blue, the Fathers' house is blue. Only the church is white, like the Pope among red cardinals. To be sure, the Municipal Building (a tiny one-story, one room bungalow with a brave big sign) is blue, too. But that's a mere accident, such as might happen when Mama buys a bolt of blue cloth at a fire sale and makes everything from Papa's shirt to Susie's hair ribbons from it, only to find one of the neighbor's children running around in blue, too. It's not quite cricket, somehow.

Something else beside blue paint we share with the Jesuit Fathers, is that old sturdy—the mission jeep. Sister Camillus rides to the commissary on Topside three mornings a week with Brother. (Her guardian angel is even now smoothing all the bumps out of her spot in Purgatory; she has had more than her share of that kind of punishment. Besides, riding with Brother in itself indicates fortitude in an heroic degree.) In addition to the commissary trips, we use the jeep for business trips, and occasionally to call on Navy friends. But we daren't call on anyone who doesn't live on a hill. Hills are important. To start the jeep, it is essential to roll downhill a bit before the motor catches on to the idea that the jeep is moving and something ought to be done about it. I got pretty agile at giving a fair-ish heave to start her rolling, and leaping aboard just as she sputters and roars at the trick played on her. We timed it pretty well, but some day someone will heave too hard, miss connections and find herself walking the long road home, unless Sister Loretta Marie can persuade Jeepie to come back for her.

It isn't hard to keep up on local news from our convent. It is right on the main road, or rather on the only road, for the others are mere foot paths. This runs along the semi-circular ridge between the ocean on the north and the bay on the south.

The life of Koror flows past the convent windows. Perhaps "flows" is not quite the word, for the roadbed would make it hard for even water to flow. Rather it would be a wild, tumbling gorge. So let's say that life jolts past the convent windows. Since the kitchen, refectory and community room (chapel, too) face the street, it's not easy to be oblivious to local happenings.

"There's the Avgas truck. I guess the plane's in from Guam already."

"A truckload of furniture just went by. That's right. I heard the Captain might be moving his office from Topside today."

"The Mogas truck! Did you know of any boat due in?"

"The bus just went by. We can get it when it comes back in a half-hour or so."

Nearly everyone waves as he goes by. Navy people in jeeps, big Palauans in trucks, women with the world-and-all on their heads, and children coming to school. It's a custom to wave to all passersby here; if you are drying a dish near a window, you wave the towel back and smile happily. These are the simplest, friendliest people in the world.

The Palauans have no last names. They are Mariana, or Artemio, or Florentina and let it go at that. They are very fond of tattooing. In the old days, they made their own tattoo ink, but the Japanese supplied them with a cheaper and better kind, so now they have forgotten how to make it. Consequently, the young people are not tattooed. However, one of the most persistent requests to the U.S. government is for tattoo ink, but so far it has not been supplied.

Women, especially, are tattooed in a dark blue which does not show up very well on their dark skins; it looks rather like a shadow or a discoloration caused by disease. But there is an intricate design if you study it. The arms, from above the elbow to the knuckles of the hand, are covered. A favorite trick is to tattoo a slender design down the calf of the leg, so that, walking behind, one thinks at first the woman is wearing stockings with a fancy seam.

The Palauan race is dying out. This is true of all the Micronesian peoples. There are few large families. In the southern islands, it is noticeable that most of the people are quite old. Within fifty years, it is estimated, the two hundred ninety people on Sonsoral shall have shrunk to about fifty.

Palauan Catholics are extremely fervent. For one thing, they have no movies to distract them, and without electricity they are spared the radio. Between seventy-five to one hundred people attend early Mass every morning; the church is filled again in the evening for rosary and night prayers. And that, from a group of three hundred Catholics on Koror, some of whom don't live too close!

At Sonsoral, there are two hundred ninety people distributed on four islands. Thirteen are pagans, the rest, Catholics. These luckless thirteen live together on one of the islands with a single Catholic to leaven the mass. Another island down there, turned in a perfect score to Father: Inhabitants, 139; Confessions 132, Baptism 1, and 6 children too young for confession; total, 139. Everyone accounted for! Yet this was the first time a priest had visited them in fourteen months, and the second time since 1940!

Kayangel, the northernmost island, has a story like Korea. When Father McManus went up there last Fall, the second time in all history that a priest had gone there, he found two Catholics. They had been baptized long ago on Koror. They were holding weekly prayer services which twenty pagans attended faithfully. Father baptized three of the twenty and held out hope for the other seventeen. Now there are five Catholics in Kayangel's one hundred and twenty inhabitants.

The least Catholic of all these islands is Pelelieu; here, on Bloody Nose Ridge, the Marines fought one of the costliest battles of the war. There are only fifty or sixty Catholics among the eight hundred people.

The power of the missionary is tremendous. His rulings are law. In a court room recently, a witness was explaining that he had told the accused not to commit the act.

"I warned him," he said, "that Padre Elias had said Catholics do not do such things."

"Was that the only reason you gave him for desisting?"

"Yes, and it should have been enough," was the firm answer.

On one of the islands, also, it is an ancient tribal ruling that no one may marry within his own clan no matter how distant the relationship may be. (Incidentally, clan membership is traced through the mother's line.) But on the whole island, there were but five clans. Besides, in two hundred ninety people, there were only five girls between the ages of ten and twenty. When Father explained the Church's law on affinity, the ancient tribal ruling was set aside without a murmur.

Spanish Capuchins came first to the islands. That was in

1891. In 1898, when Spain sold the islands to Germany, they were replaced by German Capuchins. The convent was built then and in 1911, three German Franciscan Sisters from Milwaukee came. They stayed for five years, the people told me. Not always the same Sisters, but always three. They had more than a hundred girls in a school across the road. Thirty-one stayed at the convent.

In 1916, both the German Sisters and Fathers were asked to leave when Japan took over the civil government. At the personal pressure of the Holy Father, Spanish Jesuits staffed the mission in 1921, after the islands had been five years without Mass. They built the present church, a good concrete building. White, and with a typical Spanish belfry, it has survived the war intact.

The convent was turned into a restaurant, however. Several attempts to bring Spanish Sisters here were thwarted by the Japanese. During the war, the present convent was used as Military Police Headquarters.

The last of these Spanish Jesuits were Padre Elias Fernandez and Padre Marino de la Cruz. During the war and for some years before it, the Japanese were leery of having very many Palauans on Koror; they were confined to other islands for the most part. But Padre Elias as he went from place to place told the people that the Americans would come. "This is what you must do," he said, "go forth to meet them and carry a white cloth on a stick. Do that, and they will not harm you."

In 1944, Padre Elias and Father Marino were arrested by the Kempitai (Japanese Military Police). After three months in prison on Babelthuap, they were executed together with the two priests and one Brother, missioners on Yap, and a Filipino weather observer, his Guamanian wife and three or four children who had been left behind there.

For two years there was no priest in the Palaus. Then Padre Juan Bizkarra came from Japan, with Brother John, just in time to celebrate Christmas Mass in 1946. They are Spanish Jesuits of the Toledo province; both also Basque. Father Harry Furey joined the two Basques at Koror in October, 1947. He was replaced by Father Edwin McManus, loaned from Truk, in August, 1948, and by Father Thomas Lewis in February, 1949. Father John and Brother John continued on with these.

Three Maryknoll Sisters came in September, 1948, another has come since. Once more there were Sisters in the convent, repainted and refurnished in Navy left-overs of furniture and paint.

15

The Parlor Rug
Comes Alive

WHEN I was a little tyke with pigtails, I used to stretch out on our parlor rug, stomach-down, and read the National Geographic Magazine from cover to cover. Well, if you insist on the hard truth, maybe not read every word, but every picture was gone over.

In those days, the National Geo scorned anything less civilized than a 20-foot boa constrictor coiled in the Amazon jungle, or a Bantu native with a chunk of elephant tusk stuck through his nose. Many a time, I remember jerking back in panic as I turned a page and found my hand caught in the dripping jaws of a gorilla, or the giant head of a tarantula spitting poison square at me. Indeed, my blood was so well curdled in those youthful days, nothing since has been able to make much impression.

The good old magazine took us far away in those days. Much of its lore has been forgotten. But every now and then I come across in real life, something that I recognize only because it was once in a picture I saw from the vantage point of our parlor rug. There was, for instance, the two-toed sloth on the road in Panama. We almost ran over it slowly crawling from jungle to jungle across the modern highway. "Bless us!" I thought, "I've seen you before. Ah yes, you were hanging upside down from a limb in the National Geo years ago. You're a two-toed sloth, that's what you are!"

111

I remember, too, reading about the strange idols on Easter Island and the huge cartwheels of stone which are used as money on Yap. And engraved clear in my mind is the picture of a village town-hall in the primitive South Seas—a large building of heavy planks, crudely carved and brightly painted, with a great thatched roof which was sway-backed, swooping up at the ends. But I never imagined I would ever see one.

Times have changed; the poor old world has contracted together until it's hardly worth whizzing around it. But come, you who have seen everything, come to Babelthuap, north of Koror, and revel in one of the world's last strongholds of the simple life.

But even there, we found a Sears Roebuck catalogue.

It all started most tamely. The life of Koror streams past our convent windows and waves chummily to us. Navy jeeps and ancient cars, half naked fishermen with bright blue fish on strings, women with the world-and-all on their heads—they all wave a greeting.

One day during dinner, the Koror bus, once bravely blue but now faded and venerable, groaned past, creaking, complaining and sputtering. The driver and passengers waved and we lifted our napkins to return the greeting.

"Where does that go?" I asked.

"To the ferry."

"Ferry? Ferry to what?"

"The ferry to Babelthuap, the big island just north of us."

So we decided that in the morning we would take the bus to the ferry, go to Babelthuap, look around a bit, eat a sandwich or two on Palau's biggest island (all of 22 miles long and ten miles wide!) and come right home again.

But we reckoned without Madre.

We have two girls working with us, Elena and Madre. They are the backbone of the parish. Choir rehearsals, catechism classes, evening devotions, they attend them all with such enthusiasm of Catholicity that the whole parish runs along with them. Madre particularly is a leader. When she rounds up the women to some project, they are well rounded. Elena and

Madre were to go with us on the little picnic to Babelthuap. What we did not know is that Madre's uncle is Chief Anastacio of Airai, Babelthuap's main village.

At eleven the next morning we caught the bus. Perhaps "caught" is not the right word to use; it was all too anxious to stop. The exterior was sad enough, but the interior was a revelation in decoration. Blue-flowered cotton print materials, tufted elegantly with little pompons, covered the ceiling. A six-inch wide wooden bench ran around the little tin room on wheels so that all of us passengers sat in a squarish circle, eyeing each other across the pile of fishnets, baskets of fish, banana bunches and what-not heaped in the middle—the passengers' luggage. I found myself vis-a-vis with an old Palauan wearing only a loin cloth, his wrinkled skin hanging in festoons on his aged bones. A giant green-brown crab at his feet squirmed restlessly against the bonds of strong grass which tied it securely. The old man's dusty toe was dangerously near the struggling pincher claw, but he smoked his crude pipe complacently.

The bus was an old right-hand-drive, pre-war Japanese truck chassis with a body of blue tin built on it. To start again, the driver went through the motions. He clutched the steering wheel, jiggled the clutch, tested the black bulb of his horn, and fiddled interminably with the tangle of wires which poked through the holes in his dashboard where once had been the speedometer, gauges and other instruments. With a jerk we were off.

Hanging by the strap to the steering wheel, was a lady's purse of great antiquity, gaping wide to catch the fares. It caught none from us, however; the girls could pay, but not we. The young driver shook his dark head with determination. At last, he snapped the purse shut to close the argument and we gave in. It was the Sisters' first jaunt in his Koror bus. With pride, the chariot jolted on.

The Japanese certainly did marvels on Koror. The island is surrounded by a reef where the blue-green water is perhaps 10 to 20 feet deep, but so clear that every stone and shell, every beer-can and old tire on the bottom is easily recognized.

The Japanese built up a road over this reef, stepping from

tiny island to tiny island, to the very edge of the coral shelf where it suddenly stops in a perpendicular cliff to let the deep blue channel waters go by.

A concrete dock, now sagging and broken in many places, terminates the road. Our bus driver looked hopefully to Babelthuap where a similar dock could be seen at the foot of the green hills. A few small boats bobbed in the glittering sun there, but no one was around.

The driver gave several long—excruciatingly long—blasts on his horn, squeezing every ounce of noise from the big black rubber bulb. At last, across the channel, a small boy wearing only shorts rushed on to the dock, jumped into one of the small rowboats, and started fiddling with the motor. The bus driver departed in satisfaction.

Nine of us passengers as well as the two little boys who operated it, climbed into the ferry, although it was nothing more than an over-sized rowboat with a motor in it. I sat on the edge, balancing a jovial plump Palauan on the other side. Sister Andrew Marie trailed her hand in the water as we bobbed from the light green reef water into that dark blue channel. In five minutes, again we saw a reef floor; this time it was the coral shelf which surrounds Babelthuap.

We were all for walking a bit up the rugged road which seemed to lead into plain jungle, but the curly lashes of Madre's round black eyes opened wide with surprise as she said:

"The children at Airai school are expecting you and it is too far to walk."

That settled that. From then on, Madre made the plans. Indeed, we found they had all been made overnight.

An old truck was waiting at the dock, in patient hopefulness for passengers to brave its hard benches. On this, we crept through the jungle. I watched the speedometer for several periods, and never saw it go above 5 miles per hour. So slowly did we go, that we did not need to stop for passengers; they ran after us and climbed aboard easily. It was best so, for the road was impossible. While one of the front wheels was climbing over a two-foot boulder, one of the rear ones was wallowing snugly into a two-foot hole. I felt as though we were perched on a wounded dragon slowly wriggling off to die, and stopping for a bit of gratuitous writhing now and then.

The country was wonderful to see. Deep, deep jungle, with an occasional house of nipa and split bamboo down a little pathway from the road. Mangrove swamps often lined the road; crocodiles snoozed with snouts and eyes barely visible above the dark water. Several times, big white birds with long white tails flew overhead in great wheeling swoops. Sheer cliffs of coral, crowned with trees but bare on the perpendicular faces seemed like medieval monasteries set in this paradise of green. Giant elephant ears hung like ancient shields on their stems; plumeria trees rose twenty feet high; huge ferns and old trees covered with parasitic growths filled all the interstices in view with living, struggling green. Once we passed a small bare hut, and Madre said, "That is where an American chaplain said Mass for us in 1945."

Everyone waved as we passed. Quite often, three or four old men sitting on their heels in conclave, solemnly raised their hands to us; women by the roadside straightened from bending over their taro patches; children shielded their eyes from the sun with one arm and waved the other, while the "little brown bares" ran gleefully down the road after our truck as it writhed slowly past their homes.

Almost from the very start, we could see seven large radio towers crowning a hill. After an hour, we put on a little spurt of speed and rose to the flat top of this hill. It was plain then that the towers were useless; a loose mesh of wires still connected them, however, and some strings hung helplessly beside the steel girders. Beneath and between them was the great Japanese radio station, a two-story building, roofless and crushed in many places. Our wounded dragon gave a final shudder and stopped just outside a large concrete building beside the radio station. It had once housed mighty generators and dynamos, set in great concrete troughs, but now it was the Airai school.

"Yay!" and the children tore out of school to see the Sisters.

The school is the last word in simplicity. Fair-sized tables and benches clustering around a blackboard comprise the fifth grade; middle-sized tables and benches around another blackboard, the third class; small-ish tables and benches, the second class. No attempt at partitions, no decorations, no other furniture. Several small boys had their dogs snuggling beside them on the benches. For paper, they used the pads of business forms salvaged from the old radio station. A "lesson blein" on a hanging blackboard showed, Geography, Handicraft, Farming and Nature. There was also displayed a poster showing the rhinoceros beetle's damage to the coconut trees, but, oddly enough, the poster was printed in Bengalese characters.

One of the older girls, maybe 14, sat shyly at a table twisting her lank black hair on her finger. Her skimpy middy blouse was plainly pre-war; the seams underarm were slit to accommodate her growing figure. Her dusty brown feet curled and twisted under the bench.

A large book, still in its wrapper, lay beside her. In an effort to be friendly, I said, "May I see your book?"

Giggling in an agony of embarrassment and pride, she handed me the book.

I read the wrapper. Miss Frida Ummelich, . . . with a U.S. Navy Post Office number.

"You?" I asked.

"Yes, me," she admitted. "Very many pretty pictures."

I slipped the book from the wrapper. It was the latest Sears Roebuck catalogue! I was stunned. How on earth did this child with hardly two words of English to rub together, even know about things like Sears Roebuck, much less know enough to write for a catalogue and have it sent to her across such a space of miles and longer space of civilization?

Madre soon marshalled us on.

"Will you go to the chief's house? He is expecting you."

So we climbed back into the truck with all the children. As they left the building, those children who wore shoes, carefully took them off as too sacred to wear out of school. One little girl who must have lived close by, tied her shoes together snugly. She placed her school book on her head and the shoes neatly on top of that. Balancing them lightly she ran quickly down the hillside after the troop of children.

This time, the truck crossed a long flat field on top of the mountain. It was pitted with bomb craters; Sister Camillus counted seven in easy view once. At the end, where the flatness finally gave way to the slope of mountainside, the skeleton of a plane confirmed the guess that this was formerly an airfield.

We left the truck at the almost indiscernible end of the road. The children ran ahead down the narrow trail which snaked through the tall grass and bushes on the hillside. We followed, one by one, jogging down at a fairly fast pace but with a cautious eye ever on the path to watch for unexpected gullies, roots, wash-outs or—the thought was not far from any of us—snakes.

I took several pictures of this, stepping aside to aim at the caravan strung out behind—women with bundles on their heads, men swinging big knives at their sides and Maryknoll Sisters on their first village-visitation in Palau!

Just as I snapped the last one, and rolled the film up with a sense of satisfaction at having secured some fair mission pictures, we came through a sugar cane field and saw the mission picture of the century. And I had not a single exposure left!

It was a Palauan town hall and council chamber—a big house of perhaps twenty feet wide and fifty feet long, made of heavy wooden planks set up on stilts and approached by stones piled before the front door in crude steps. The roof was nipa and swooped up at each end. On the triangular gables thus formed at the front and back was any number of carvings, painted in yellow, white and black. At first we just gasped at the multiplicity of figures in childish scrawls all over the surface, as if some giant, waiting for a phone call, had doodled away an hour or so, using the house front as a telephone pad.

"Look, it tells a story!" cried Sister Loretta Marie.

It was real picture writing—and of very modern events. Airplanes buzzed and whirled and dive-bombed above. You could see a truck climbing uphill. Many men were running away frantically while other figures were left behind, prone on the ground. Over in a corner, several men crouched in a bomb-shelter dug into the hillside. Others were carrying someone away in either a stretcher or a coffin. And way up in the apex of the roof, sure enough, an American flag with crude figures "1944." It commemorated, Madre said, the first bombing of Babelthuap.

We examined the house thoroughly, and wept that we had no film left.

Stepping from stone to stone of the pile heaped in front, we mounted to the front door—or rather to the small opening no higher than 3 feet and no wider than 2, which was the only entrance. Inside was a large bare room with more gaudily painted red and yellow carvings on every rafter, mostly just rows of heads of primitive proportions, eyes set too close together, small forehead, huge ears with earrings dangling on long strings. These faces were everywhere. The inside of the roof with its even rows of nipa was beautiful. At every place where the roof joined the upright posts, was a carved board protruding like a shelf into the room, covered with bright painted carvings. The general effect of looking along each side of the room where these shelf-like things protruded was similar to seeing gargoyles on the columns of a cathedral, one after the other in regular sequence. Some people must sleep there, for several sleeping mats, neatly rolled up, were stowed on top of these shelves, wedged for security against the angle of the roof.

The floor was made of great planks, polished and shiny. If they had been fitted together more smoothly, they would have made a fine ballroom floor. Set in the floor, were two neat squares of earth, built up from under the house to the exact level of the floor. These provided cooking space. There were the remnants of a small fire on one.

Everything in the house was beautifully clean. This is most impressive in these people. The children have fine sturdy legs, no scars of previous sores, no present ones. There are no babies with scrofulous heads and running eyes as in China and the Philippines; the children's teeth are white and firm although the older people's are black with betel nut chewing. Occasionally, a child may need urgent attention from a handkerchief, but that happens in the best of families everywhere, I guess. Even the toilets are primitive but very clean.

As we stepped down from the house, Madre showed us the outdoor conference rostrum nearby where inter-village agreements are reached. Stones make a sort of raised circular platform, maybe a foot higher than the surrounding ground. Two larger stones in the center face each other; these are seats for the chiefs of the respective villages. They alone make the decision, but at a respectful distance are other stones in a crude circle where the headmen of the villages await announcement of the decision. When the conference between chiefs is over, one of them goes over to a stone lectern (really, it looks like a lectern, a tall stone topped by a large flat stone, slightly tilted) and informs the villagers of the decision reached.

We looked at everything, sitting on all the stones, examining the lectern. And right beside the chief's seat, wedged between the rocks, was an old Lucky Strike cigarette wrapper.

The road from here on, was very interesting. It was a path of stones, raised about six inches from the ground, and about six feet wide. Most of the stones were rounded, of course, but down the center of this wide pathway, was a strip of flattened stones. Whether they had been flattened by use, or by artificial means, I do not know. We walked some two miles down this roadway. It was difficult walking, for one had to watch each step to plant his feet correctly on the next stone.

We came to a crossroad where four such broad stone pathways met. A neat circular bench of raised stones here invited rest. This is the center for the four villages of the Airai district. We took the road to the left, leading down to the sea.

Soon we stepped off the road to Anastacio's house. It befitted a chief—large, roofed with corrugated tin, and wide open to all comers. Anastacio himself, an old man with white hair and a white mustache which contrasted oddly with his brown skin, hurried forward. He was dressed in khaki shorts and a faded blue denim shirt. Even the collar was fastened tight in our honor. He was a dear. He raised our hands to his forehead in respect, smiled his betel-blackened smile and led us to a table, covered with a white cloth, set up inside the house.

The entire entourage of some fifty-or-so children and about ten adults came with us. The house itself was absolutely bare; it was more like a pavilion, open on every side, with a beautifully polished floor, raised about two feet from the ground. What might be called a center aisle was a trough on the ground-level which extended more than halfway into the house from the front door. Here, ordinarily, one left his shoes before stepping up on to the polished floor. But they would not permit us to remove our shoes.

They brought fried bananas, and candied cassava (tapioca), and fresh bananas. Each of us had her own coconut full of coconut juice; the top had been deftly cut off and we drank from the whole coconut as from a large mug. Our own unpretentious ham sandwiches and cookies were lost in this banquet, so we presented most of them ceremonially to the chief as he sat cross-legged on the floor behind us. Later his wife, Anastacia (we could not find out if she was Anastacia because she was married to Anastacio or if she had always had that name) came in and she too was presented with ham sandwiches.

As we rose to leave, Anastacio made a little speech interpreted by Madre. He was honored, he said, that the Sisters' first visit to Babelthuap should be to his village and his house. Sisters Loretta Marie, Camillus and Andrew Marie replied in their brand-new Palauan and I said, "Arigato gozaimas" (meaning "thank you"), glad that study in Japanese war years was not entirely fruitless.

Beside the chief's house, was another pavilion-like place in which quite a few women were sitting cross-legged on the floor. Several wore Palauan money on strings around their necks. No one knows for sure what it is made of, but a geologist here recently said it might be old Chinese pottery. It looks like broken arcs of a circle of hard yellow material; pieces of various lengths are strung lengthwise on red string and worn fairly tight around the neck. A little girl in the truck beside me had such a piece. I thought I might get it for the museum at Maryknoll but the mother, interpreted through Madre, said it was worth $100 American money. Father McManus says, too, that they will not give nor sell it to foreigners.

I think that most of those who wear Palauan money are not Christian. The little girl was not, and the women who wore it in the pavilion did not smile nor wave at us. All the other people, men and women and children, wore medals around their necks. The village of Airai is Christian to a large percent.

We then went to visit Clara. The entourage of 50 barefoot children went, too. As we strung across the fields or passed the small patches of sugar cane, taro or tapioca the sun glared on us. It was about one o'clock then.

Clara has been ill with tuberculosis for two years now. She lives by herself in a tiny, immaculate houselet on a small cliff overlooking the bluest-greenest reef you can imagine. Even Hawaii can boast no better view than from Clara's little house. Madre and we four Sisters went inside, and there was barely room to kneel. Clara lay on a spotless mattress-like pad on the floor, very thin, very weak, speaking in whispers while the tears flowed down her cheeks. The house is practically lined with holy cards.

It seems that Clara was always a good Christian but she was forced to marry a pagan. Two years ago when she became ill, she asked to be relieved of this marriage that she might return to the sacraments and "be sorry for her sins." Her brother and his good wife built this shelter for her and take care of her. One could not imagine a better place for a TB patient. Sun and air come in on all four sides; the tiny room was immaculate; quietness or cheerful companionship was hers in alternate doses. One felt oneself in the presence of real holiness with Clara. It was plain she was beloved of all the village. The women and children with us leaned in at the windows, just looking at her.

On the way back to the road, we rested in the shade of a huge tree. We four Sisters sat on a board about three inches from the ground. Everyone else squatted on his heels or rested on stones in a big ring around. The children were friendly but shy. Language difficulties kept me pretty quiet, but the other Sisters put the time to good use learning new words and confirming tentative definitions of old ones.

We walked back the two miles or so to where the truck waited for us at the end of the bombed-out airfield. The entire troupe of children boarded it with us and rode all the tortuous way down to the ferry, over that jungle road, two good hours of squirming and writhing. I think we slowly wriggled over every rock we had met on the way up and found others as well. But at the end when Sister tried to pay for fares both ways and the three hour wait as well, Madre protested, "Chief Anastacio has said, 'You will not buy the truck.'"

Orders from Anastacio were meant to be obeyed. We could not persuade them to take a penny.

JAPAN

16

Picture in Reverse

I HAD a funny feeling in Japan that I had lived through all
this before—the long lines shuffling forward to get rations of rice;
the shabby, run-down-at-the-heels clothing; the charcoal-run
buses ludicrously overstuffed with passengers; the appraising
glance that children dropped into every garbage can; the pa-
thetic vivacity of girls clinging to soldiers' arms.

Surely, it was all very familiar.

Then it came back. Oh yes, that was Manila during the war,
when Japanese troops occupied it; this is Japan with Americans.
Occupied countries have features in common, no matter who
does the occupying.

Japan's trouble is not that anything is being taken out of the
country, but that so many people have been poured into it. In
all the Orient you find no Japanese ex-patriates; Manchuria,
Korea, and former Pacific Island possessions such as the Mari-
anas, Yap and Palau have been emptied completely. The Philippines and China are not yet healthy climates for Japanese.
Merchants and government officials who formerly carried Japan's
trade and empire everywhere, are home now, squeezing desperately into a country that has always been too small for its
energetic population.

The result is what you would expect.

The doorbell rang at our convent in Kyoto one morning. The

girl on the doorstep stared with sullen eyes for a heavy moment
—long enough for me to appraise her straggly hair, her shoddy
kimono and bare feet in wooden shoes.

"Can you give me something to live for?" she asked at last.

Once, she had been nice-looking, and fairly well-to-do. But
1945 saw her parents killed and her home destroyed. The same
bomb sent her to a hospital for a year, and so disfigured her that
her fiance called off their engagement. She went downhill very
fast after that. Then the movie, "The Bells of Saint Mary's,"
came to Japan, and she saw it.

"If anybody can help me," she said, "it's the Catholic
Church."

With that, she came to us.

Hiroku is another.

A Maryknoll Father brought her to us. "She came from
Tokyo alone and has spent a week in Kyoto roaming the streets.
Talks of suicide all the time; all she needs is kindness, I think."

She was tractable enough all that day, but the next morning
she was gone. "Thanks for your kindness," a little note said, "but
it's no use."

We prayed like everything through the day. Dear Lord!
Where could she be? What was she doing? "We got her too late,
I guess," we told each other as we met outside the chapel door,
from time to time.

But late that night she came back, a drab little figure under
the gate-lamp as I opened the door.

"I tried and tried. Five times I tried to jump into Lake Biwa
. . . I couldn't, that's all."

Hiroku still hasn't told us her story. Some day, perhaps, she
will. In the meantime, she warbles and chirps, happy as a bird
while she mans the business end of a broom, or splashes gaily in
the laundry suds. It's only sometimes in chapel that you see the
heavy cloud of memories come over her bright eyes.

But despair has not gripped all of Japan's youth. There's a
tremendous rush for the new ideas, too. Sister Veronica Marie
and I were caught one day in that rush.

Two college boys, with blue students' caps pushed back on

THE AGE-OLD TREES AT ISE, JAPAN'S MOST SACRED SPOT, BEAR
THEIR CENTURIES WITH DIGNITY.

HARUKO-SAN WAS EASY TO MAKE FRIENDS
WITH—BUT THE TEMPLE DANCING GIRLS
WERE FORMAL AND ALOOF.

CHOPSTICKS AND BOY-SIZE APPETITES SOON
EMPTY THE LITTLE TIN LUNCHBOXES.

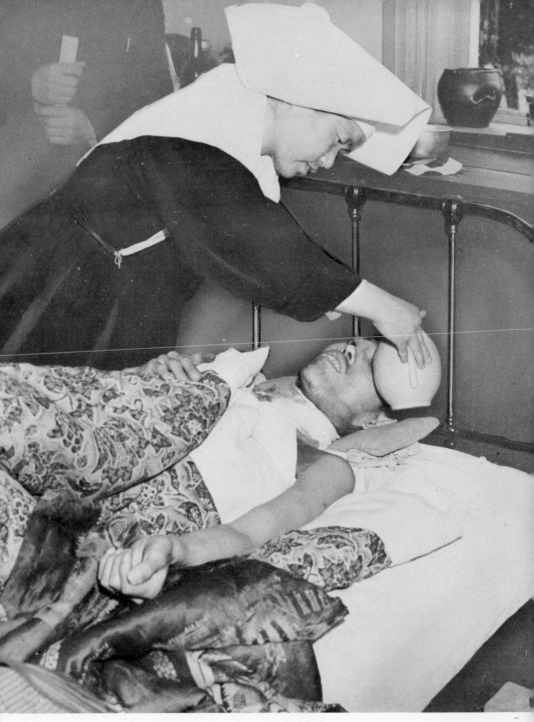

Waters of Baptism bring Life to a dying soul. This Korean St. Paul de Chartres Sister is a doctor.

IN THE QUONSET CONVENT ON GUAM, YOU CAN'T SURPASS THAT OLD
SOUTHE'N HOSPITALITY.

STARVATION AND LEPROSY, THE AGE-OLD SCOURGES OF MANKIND.

 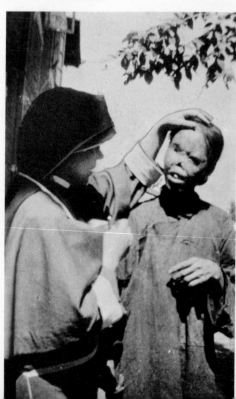

their foreheads, were stewing over their English lesson in the streetcar. As we sat beside them, they gave each other a look that spoke volumes. The English battle was won for the day.

They stood politely, doffed their caps and bowed. "Please, Miss, will you explain this word?" One word led to another; the lesson was done in jig time. Then they started reciting. "Four score and seven years ago . . ." was followed by "When in the course of human events . . ." and the entire Star Spangled Banner. But we were on a two-hour run from Kyoto to Nara, and no formal English lesson can last that long. They fired the first gun.

"You belong to the new religion," they said, as a passive statement of obvious fact.

"New religion!" (Sister Veronica Marie's Irish was up.) "Two thousand years new! The Catholic Church isn't new! Truth never changes."

It was odd, how that last sentence caught one of the boys. He had been the most talkative, but now he lapsed into thought, saying "Truth never changes!" very quietly to himself. I was fascinated looking at him. It was as if Sister had injected a shot of God's grace under his skin as she said the terse sentence and I could watch it permeate his brain like a color spreading through cloth.

Conversation died down and I was afraid we had been too abrupt. They talked together in Japanese for a few minutes and turned to us. (Oh, it was a very formal invitation, indeed, and would probably have taken their last nickel!)

"It has been pleasant indeed to meet you, Misses," the bright lad said in a style copied from Learn-English-in-Three-Weeks textbooks. "We would like this to ripen to a beautiful friendship. Will you accompany us to the movies this evening?"

"Better come to see us next Sunday," Sister said with a smile.

They did, surprisingly enough. The next Sunday, and the next Sunday, and the next one, too. Before I left, they were going to Mass as well, and practising English from the Catechism. And that is the beginning of the end, you know.

Another time, a tinkle of the bell at the foot of the cloister stairs called Sister Veronica Marie to the parlor to greet a young man of the neighborhood. He was a student of the University, Sister knew.

"Good day, Sister," he said very formally, with a bow. "I have come to borrow a book."

"Certainly, if we have it," Sister said. "But I'm afraid we wouldn't have any textbook you would need."

"No, not a textbook," he answered. "I wish to borrow a book about God. I am interested, very interested, in God."

Again, there was the strenuous morning I spent with two bumptious young boys. About 13 or 14 years old, they had a glorious time pealing our convent bell. They grinned triumphantly at each other as I opened the door. "See, it works!" they said.

"We just came to look around and see what a convent is," they introduced themselves.

Smiling inside and out, I took them around the house—garden, kitchen, parlor, dog house, tool shed, music room. I was thinking of how two American youngsters might feel if some Shinto priestess, recently moved to town, were to conduct them around her home. Why, they would be heroes in the neighborhood for weeks.

We came to the foot of the stairs leading to our sleeping rooms. They had one foot on the bottom stair, ready to investigate further.

"Sorry, but visitors are not allowed up there," I said.

They looked their disappointment, but decided it would be all right with them.

Into the chapel! They turned their necks from one corner of the large quiet room to the other. The rice-straw matting on the floor, the large flat cushions to kneel on, the little shelf of books, the flickering sanctuary lamp, the tabernacle veiled with gold lace—they missed nothing.

"Kirei na!" The equivalent in English would be "Pretty nice, eh?"

In the music room, they shouted for joy over the piano. Right then and there, they would start taking lessons. "Right here! Right away! Sister, please teach us!"

"So sorry, boys, not today."

The two left, happy with some hard candy in their cheeks. I was so tempted to follow them to the corner to see if their friends were there, eager to hear all about the adventure with the strange American women!

I was stunned by the shabbiness of Japan. I refer to the Japanese Japan; Americans in Japan ride in shiny buses and good trains, they shop in modern stores, they dress in West Point khaki. But all these niceties are labeled "Occupation Personnel Only." It is not unjust; indeed it is a help to Japan that we bring our own transportation and our own food. At least, we do not deprive them of what little they have—Americans do not constitute other mouths to feed. Nonetheless, it is hard to see such glittering victory beside the shabby defeat.

For the most part, we Maryknoll Sisters ride with the Japanese. What trains! The plush seating has worn through, and hangs in tatters or has been replaced by burlap. Some seats are gone entirely, to allow for more standing passengers. The windows are broken and wooden boards keep out the winter cold— and the light, too. Tin strips do their best to cover the cracks. And yet the amenities are preserved; after he has collected his tickets, the conductor faces his shabby carful and, in thanks, politely doffs his cap to all. Then he vanishes into the next car to do the distasteful business of collecting money there.

The city buses are, often, run by charcoal. A big thing like the hot water heater in our home long ago, hangs precariously on the rear end of the bus, huffing and puffing like an old man out of breath, trying perpetually to catch up with the shoddy bus. Nonetheless, as the ancient thing crawls to the curb to pick up the passengers, the woman conductor sings out to the waiting crowd, "Oh, so sorry to have kept you waiting!" and stands back as they jam past her. I was always expecting to hear someone answer, "You're no sorrier than we are."

Everyone who boasts a pair of foreign shoes has fitted the sole with iron cleats. (The racket a single altar boy can make changing the book at Mass makes one think a football team is scrambling up and down the steps.) Children's shoes are slit around the toe to permit their feet to grow. It's common to see a big toe overhanging the sole as a child runs down the street. Dresses are skimpy and plain. No longer do women wear the gay flowered kimono for ordinary wear. It's too expensive. Until Japan's silk mills can get on their feet, Japanese women will wear American clothes.

"I can make two American dresses from one of my old kimonos," one woman told me. "Now I'm down to my last kimono, and I had nearly fifty before the war!"

The Japanese, you know, can grow anything, anywhere. They have to, now, when the food situation is as it is. In June, the ripe wheat spreads out of the fields, running up the incline of the railway bed, and stops only a few inches from the tracks. In harvesting, the men step aside to let the train pass, and then close in to work. Wheat grows up to the steps of a man's home; it waves down the river banks to the very edge of the water. It grows in pots and wooden boxes. It straggles through the cracks of a broken pavement.

On a Monday, we rode the burlap seats of an ancient railway car from Kyoto to Tsu. It was a trip of four hours through wheat harvesting scenes. Women, in wide baggy pants gathered at the ankles, strode through the grain carrying armfuls of golden stalks, to where a man operated a threshing and winnowing machine, hitched to a gasoline motor. Over all, the sun beat down on bone-dry ground. Only a tiny spot of vivid green here and there showed where the seedling riceplants dabbled their feet in water-filled paddies.

On Thursday, we returned to Kyoto over the same route. But this time, the fields were great seas of mud. The women had rolled up their pants' legs and stood knee-deep in water. Each was bent at a right angle, thrusting green shoots deep into the soft mud. A Filipino ditty ran through my head incessantly:

> "Planting rice is no fun;
> Work all day 'til set of sun.
> Cannot stand, cannot sit,
> Cannot rest for a little bit."

But the marvel was, there had not been a drop of rain from the sun-baked Monday to Thursday. The Japanese irrigation system is responsible; Japanese civic sense welds the nation together. They know so well how to work together for the common good.

A smattering of Japanese picked up in Manila during the war, made me a traffic hazard on the streets of Occupied Japan. The temptation to read the Katakana signs to see just what new quirks the English language could be twisted into for the benefit of the Occupation forces, was usually too great to resist. At first the Sisters took me gently by the arm and tried to distract me; then they insisted that I hold on to their clothes in some way, so as not to get lost in crowds. But in time, they learned to let me puzzle out the sign and enjoy my little joke, before proceeding across any main thoroughfare.

Katakana is a syllable-phonetic language. Instead of each sound being represented by a letter as is the case with European languages, in this phonetic system each syllable has a character. Ka, ke, ku, ki, ko are five entirely different characters; so are ba, be, bi, bo, and bu, and ya, ye, yi, yo, and yu. That is where the fun comes in. The system was devised to spell out foreign words, since in Oriental languages, the symbol for a word has no relation at all to its sound. It is also the baby-writing in Japan; it's easier than the kanji of real characters. Children learn first to write in Katakana; then they go on to Hiragana (another phonetic system). Finally they learn the kanji which are Chinese characters with Japanese pronunciations and meaning.

In English we like to pile a lot of consonants together; the Japanese string them all out with a vowel between. We usually like a good strong consonant at the end of a word; but the Japanese usually put a "u" at the end, just to make it softer. As a result, they eat hamu and so-sah-ji (sausage) and drink sah-i-da (cider) and are valiantly trying to use a knife-u and fork-u at the taboru (table). Also, they read the American magazines, Ti-mu and Li-fu.

All over Japan, but particularly thick around army billets

and public parks, are shabby looking men bearing banners, red with white lettering.

"These must be pickets," I thought. "Probably Communists protesting the occupation, or somebody else with a grievance."

"Ah-ee-su ku-ree-mu." They were ice-cream peddlers haunting the places for best customers! Not far from them was the man selling that well-known American delicacy, the Hah-to dahgu. And across the street was a bee-ru hah-ru (beer hall).

More than American foods have percolated through Japan. The ads even in streetcars which were definitely off-limits to American soldiers spoke in garish characters of pah-ma-ne-to way-bu for the straight black hair. (And to think, wavy hair was once a disgrace in Japan!) The night clubs advertise "bu-gi wu-gi"; the drug stores sell mee-ru-ku say-kee (that's a hard one; it's "milk-shake"). "R" is always substituted for "L" (which the Japanese find impossible to pronounce). In Tokyo, one may ride the esu-cu-ray-ta (escalator) from floor to floor of the day-pah-to, or Department Store.

The Japanese have always liked foreign words; they have absorbed more of our way than other Oriental peoples. In 1938, when I made a short visit to Japan, the street signs and railroad station notices were written twice, once in Japanese, once in English. American movies played in the big cities without bothering about translation, although a written explanation ran alongside the screen. Even then, any number of people were anxious to try out their English on any foreign face.

Even in 1938 the people of Japan were suffering from war. At the railroad station at Yokohama we ran into a huge crowd of women in sombre kimonos. (It's a really serious occasion when the gay butterfly kimonos are laid aside for grey or dark blue; I don't think I have ever seen a plain black kimono.) They gathered on the square before the station, perhaps 300 saddened women and, while a military band played lugubriously, each received a small box of ashes, all that remained of the man she had sent to the war in China.

In Tokyo, a woman came to see me, because she had heard that I lived in the Philippines during the war.

"Do something for my husband, Sister," she begged. "He is

under a death sentence in the Philippines as a war criminal. They say he bayonetted a little girl of ten years, many times, and then hacked her head off with a bolo.

"The only evidence against him is the mother's testimony and identification. He did not do it, he says, but another Japanese did, and he is willing to die to expunge the wrong. But, Sister, it is down to this, a Filipina's word against a Japanese man's word. Of course the mother is believed; but at such a time of stress it is hard to see how she could be so positive in her identification. My husband is supported only by other Japanese, who know he was not in the vicinity at the time."

Of course, she was grasping at a straw to think I could help, poor woman.

It was Augustine Okano's sister-in-law who told me the finish of *his* story. Augustine was a splendid Catholic, an officer of the Religious Section of the Japanese Army in Manila. We knew him quite well.

Okano died of dysentery in the mountains of Luzon, but his wife heard that he had been murdered by his own men, because he had been friendly to the priests and religious in Manila. "Was this true?" she wrote and asked me. I was happy to tell his sister-in-law that it was not. I could not see his wife because—she had entered the Spanish Mercedarian Order and was getting ready for Profession.

"They had been married only a month," the sister-in-law said, "and had often talked of separating to enter religious life. In Augustine's last letter, he heartily agreed to it. But God had something better for him; he was to enter Eternal Life."

If you ever want to realize down to your inmost bones, the supra-nationality of the Church, just manage to get yourself made a prisoner-of-war. In Tokyo, it was Old Home Week, greeting Japanese friends who had helped us when we were under them in Manila.

At the entrance to the Fushimi-Dai convent, a young Sister gasped as she opened the door for us. Her bright eyes danced as she held out her hands. "Oh Sister!"

"Do you know the Maryknoll Sisters?" I asked, thinking she recognized the habit, not me.

"I know *you!*"

She was a little tease; she wouldn't tell me where I had known her for a long time.

"I was Kawakami San," she confessed at last. "During the war the army sent me to Manila to teach Japanese. Don't you remember? You were one of my pupils!"

Sure enough. While interned, we had several nice Japanese girls assigned to teach us Japanese.

"And when did you enter the convent?" I asked.

"Two days after I landed back in Japan."

You never know what's stirring in the mind of even the most innocent-looking people, do you! Who would have known she had that desperate plan up her kimono sleeve?

17

Lady Luck at Ise

LADY LUCK was with me at Ise.

Or, to put a more Christian tone to this, my Guardian Angel probably ran ahead to the famous Ise shrine and fixed things up for me to see some of the inner workings of Shintoism. Certainly, he was not around right before breakfast; I broke my glasses, a major calamity indeed since I can't even hear what people say without my glasses.

But for all that, he is splendidly forgiven; he took us into more Japanese religious ceremonial, dancing and music than most visitors see in a million years in Japan.

To start with, I went with the right people—two of them, and both Maryknoll Sisters. Twenty-some years ago, a Japanese teacher in Korea threw down Buddha to become a Catholic. She was a fervent young woman and wanted to dedicate her life to bringing others into the Church. The answer to that ambition was to come all the way to the States and become a Maryknoll Sister. Sister Sabina has had a hair-raising life ever since. All through the war years she stayed in Dairen, Manchuria, going short on food, sleep and warmth. But that was nothing to the few years after, when Russia helped herself to all of Manchuria and northern Korea. Then the shoe really pinched. There was constant spying, sudden alarms, raids, and nights spent on the sacristy floor, confiding to Our Lord the bodies of the virgins dedicated to Him.

Nothing of that sort can daunt the old Maryknoll spirit, however. Every minute possible was spent in teaching, instructing, and baptizing. Three years of that, and she returned to Japan.

I met Sister Sabina at Tsu. Thin, wiry, intense, a mere wisp of a person! But stacked in that small head is a wealth of information on her beloved Japan—its ancient religions, its culture, its fascinating history. As a missioner, she is as intrepid as Daniel Boone and as wily as Ulysses. She has groups of high-school teachers, groups of nurses and interns, groups of poor women, groups of patients at the local tuberculosis sanatorium, all learning to love Christ as she does. She revels in Japan's movement to the Church; there's no holding her down while souls are waiting to be harvested.

Sister Paul Miki has lived the other side of the story. She was born a pagan in Los Angeles and grew up so. In the American internment camps in Arizona, where Japanese-Americans were herded for the war years, she met the Catholic Church. She, too, became a Maryknoll Sister and is now in Japan, struggling manfully to learn the language which suits her face.

As you see, I went off to Japan's Sacred Spot well fortified with ancient Japanese culture on the one hand, and Nisei California on the other.

Ise is the cradle of the Japanese nation. It seems that the goddess Amaterasu-Omikani came to earth here. When she left for heaven again, her grandson remained to begin the Japanese race, just as Romulus and Remus began Rome and Adam and Eve started the whole thing off. At parting, she gave him three gifts—a mirror, a sword and a necklace. The sword is kept in another temple up north; the necklace is handed down from Emperor to Emperor; the mirror is at Ise.

As the umptieth great-great-great-grandson of the Goddess, the Emperor has responsibilities to her. He has to report any event of national importance in person. I read in the Manila papers of 1942 that he reported the fall of Singapore and later that of Bataan and Corregidor. I never thought then, to see a sign at Ise informing all who read English that MacArthur expected all service men to respect the sanctity of the place. In other words, not to treat it like a picnic ground.

It used to be that the eldest daughter of the Emperor lived a virgin life here in seclusion as custodian of the shrine. Of late centuries, however, some feminine member of the Imperial family, not necessarily a virgin, is charged with its care. The Princess Kitashirakawa, daughter of the late Emperor and auntie of the present one, is in charge now. And we had the good luck to run right into her!

Ise is my idea of a natural heaven. Great trees—giants, hundreds of years old. Tremendous trunks, sweeping branches, noble crowns lost in clouds above. Wide gravel paths, fish ponds where the huge gold fish glint lazily among the water lily pads, and everything is exquisitely clean. I looked for rusted beer cans in the fish ponds, for cigarette stubs in the gravel and candy wrappers in the bushes. We couldn't find even a pop-bottle in all of Ise's five square miles or more of magnificent groves. And we thank God for that.

Folks have a nice habit of donating their best cocks to Ise. Like the doves of Capistrano Mission in California, they come around the visitors quite chummily. Two of the Emperor's white horses have permanent residence at Ise, too. "White Snow" and "Aged Frost" wear the Imperial Chrysanthemum with sixteen petals on their blankets. In honorable retirement, they thoughtfully chew the best oats in Japan and dream with lacklustre eyes of the celestial stalls where Emperors they have carried come to visit with sugar in their palms.

We had walked, absolutely alone in this Garden of Eden, in the cloister quiet of ancient trees, when a policeman stepped forth suddenly from the side of the path.

"You can't go any further," he said. "Prince and Princess are at their morning prayers at the shrine." He pointed to a small log-cabin sort of place, surrounded by a high-ish fence of young saplings. But the roof-ends swooped up in a blaze of gold leaf and the ridge-pole gleamed in the spatters of sun which sifted through the trees.

As he spoke, two ladies in quiet grey kimonos came out and

faced the entrance. Then two priests in great long kimonos with wide sleeves, walked out on great thick lacquer shoes and stood waiting respectfully, too. We were the only other people in sight, so we backed up to the side of the wide gravel pathway and waited to see what would happen next.

In a moment or two, four sharp handclaps sounded from inside the log-cabin shrine. Their Highnesses also emerged slowly in procession. Guards, priests, ladies-in-waiting formed an escort and the whole entourage started down the path toward us—a wide procession with everyone keeping at least ten feet from everyone else, so that the ten or twelve of them spread out over the wide pathway. Nobody spoke; they walked solemnly, deep in prayer.

The Princess came first, a woman about sixty, tall, spare, and dressed strangely in white foreign dress of about the 1910 era. Then the High Priest in full white kimono and heavy lacquer shoes; a ceremonial headdress with high curled top-piece like a question mark, bobbed over his head. Finally the Prince, dressed also as a priest.

They advanced slowly toward us in dignified silence. We felt like such yokels standing there, gaping at the strange religious dress of ancient Japan. Sister Sabina first, and then we two Americans, bowed politely to the Princess and she dipped her head slightly to us. I had the unbroken lens of my glasses held up to the one eye that could function. This, and trying to operate a camera, gave me more than enough to do. I was still fumbling with frames and the lens and gadgets on the camera as the white-muffled figures dwarfed smaller and smaller beneath the ancient trees. And I hadn't enough brash Americanism in me to run after and tell them to stop!

We fell into another piece of good fortune further on, at the big temple and the sacred dance floor, a great heavy hulk of a building with cumbrous swooping roof. Many people were here in bright kimonos and gay sunshades; little children tugging at their mamas to come look at the turtle in the pond, or chasing after the handsome cocks with their iridescent neck feathers and golden eyes.

I suppose we must have been conspicuously drab in that crowd. At any rate, a priest in light blue pleated skirt came toward us from a sort of rectory-like effect beside the temple. He must have been posted to be so excruciatingly polite to Americans that bumptious G.I.'s would not have the nerve to climb over fences to the inner shrine or peep through the heavy white curtains of the sacred places. Mine was the only foreign face in the park, just then, so we got the full benefit of his attention.

He led us back through the priests' house to a tiny room fitted in foreign fashion with a simple table covered with green velvet. We had tea from a temple serving maid, dressed in Amaterasu's red and white livery. Of course, we signed the guest book, right under a major general from Tokyo who had come yesterday.

"A temple ceremony is about to begin. Would you care to see it?"

He led us through some more corridors, past a small dancing chamber to the main temple dance room. We stooped under two huge magnificent dark blue curtains bearing the Imperial Chrysanthemum and caught up by heavy orange tassels. The large room before us was divided in half by a low railing. On our side was the place for the people, covered with tatami. The priest looked at me, decrepit foreigner that I was, and whispered to Sister Sabina.

"Do you want a chair," she said, "or can you sit on the floor like us?"

"Of course I can sit on the floor!" I said, and kneeling, sat back on my heels just as if it didn't hurt at all.

Beyond, was the dance floor, gleaming in the glow of two half-columns of smoky fire on either side of the altar, a simple high table of fragile wood built into a shallow alcove. It was absolutely bare, waiting for the gift to be placed on it. Flanking the altar were two great easels draped with broad streamers of silk in the five sacred colors—white, purple, orange, red and green. A round mirror surmounted one easel; a sword, the other.

"Not a soul around but us!" I thought at first, but soon a little blob of something dark resolved itself into the figure of a little old man in foreign dress, quietly sitting back on his heels right in front of the dance floor. He was the donor of the gift soon to be presented at the dance.

A gong sounded deep outside. A man stalked in solemnly in dark green stiff kimono and question-mark hat. He carried a branch of green leaves in his hand and ceremoniously dusted off the donor who huddled down closer to the floor as the leaves swished back and forth over him. Thus was he purified before his gift could be presented.

Five musicians came in and seated themselves, gonging and thrumming quietly. Now came four dancing girls in high gilt headdress and long white kimonos over red trousers, the legs of which trailed behind them, as they teetered in with mincing steps. Two other girls carried in several round boxes like the old-fashioned hat boxes, and placed them on the altar.

The dancing girls were as much interested in us as we were in them. Like altar boys at a High Mass, all during the ceremonies they couldn't resist a glance now and then at us three Sisters sitting on our heels alone in the congregation.

The musicians really went to it, then. A high shriek like an air-raid siren at top level, then a drop in pitch and up again, whined in agony. Higher and higher it mounted, and the drum rumbled fast behind it, as the priest entered majestically. He was all in white; the great curls of his headdress made solemn jerks as he advanced across that gleaming floor to the altar. The frenzied music sounded like a soul in torment high above us all; the drums thundered and rolled. I was scared; surely the Old Boy could not be far away; I made the Sign of the Cross.

Suddenly, the racket stopped, like a cliff of sound which moves away and leaves one hanging in mid-air. Everyone huddled close to the floor—musicians, dancing girls, the donor, and the friendly guide beside us. (We felt like Protestants at Benediction.) The high-priest also dropped to his knees and bent double over the floor before the altar. He prayed aloud to Amaterasu. We caught her name at the beginning, just as you can often catch "Deus qui . . ." at the start of the Collect. It was a long prayer. Finally he rose, clapped his hands four times, then four times more, and once again, nine times in all. He bowed and walked slowly out in deep silence. No one had moved from utter prostration.

Now followed the real dance. The four girls formed a square, facing the altar, arms outstretched so that the wide kimono sleeves (much wider than ordinary ones) completely hid their hands. In the right hand was a branch of green leaves, symbol of the goddess. The movements were slow and dignified, very graceful without at any time being sprightly. They met and parted, waved the branches, raised one arm and lowered the other, took a step forward and one back, and often sank on their two knees, but never once turning completely around so that their backs would be to the altar.

We could see, as they danced, that the red trousers were made very big, so that the crotch came about six inches from the floor and the dancers moved their feet in what would be the knees or higher. Thus two long trains of red silk followed each dancer gracefully. The priest with us explained that this was to prevent their feet from ever touching the sacred floor. These girls are virgins: "It would be an insult to the goddess if she were served by any other," the priest said.

The dance over, the dancing girls removed the gifts from the altar, gave them to the two girls who had carried them in. The musicians and dancers slowly departed and the two lesser girls brought to the old man in front of us, a scroll acknowledging his gift. "He can hang it in his front room now," the priest said. Then he turned to me, "I shall ask the dancing girls to come out in front where you can take their pictures; it's too dark in here," he said. Outside, two of the dancers waited for us. They were very accommodating, but quite reserved. They stood anywhere I put them and posed with Sisters Sabina and Paul Miki. But never a smile or friendly gesture.

Our friendly priest in the white kimono and blue pleated skirt now said, "I will conduct you to the inner shrine." We went up the gravel road a way and mounted a broad stone stairway. Here were three thatched houses with golden logs on the roofs and high antique gable ends. The inmost one, where reposes the original mirror given by the goddess to her grandson, has an entire roof-ridge of gold. As we passed the first white curtain where many worshippers were bowing, clapping their hands in prayer and offering gifts, I had high hopes that we would be taken to see the real mirror. But our guide only took us around to the side where we could look over a low fence made of plain wood, unpainted. We could not see much, only a vacant field and another plain broad fence beyond that. It was all extremely simple, even drab, except for the ornate roofing.

For two thousand years the Ise shrine has been a sacred spot; some of the trees are seven and eight hundred years old. Yet the buildings which house its most sacred object are square little blocks with thatch on top which can be torn down and re-built with very little trouble.

Sister Sabina set to work on our guide with an invitation to visit our church at Tsu. "This is the center of Japan's religious life," she explained later to us. "If we can convert Ise, all Japan would follow."

All in all, the Maryknoll vicariate here is the toughest assignment in Japan. Not only does it hold the center of Shintoism, but of Buddhism as well. Nara is called the Rome of Buddhism; the oldest, largest and most influential temple is not far from our tiny convent. Kyoto, two hours from Nara, is the administrative center for Buddhism. There are many, many temples throughout the city. Well, our Sisters can take it!

KOREA

18

"Le Cheep"

IT'S a poor convent, indeed, that can't afford a pet. Nearly everyone I know has some stray on which to lavish affectionate forgiveness. It may be a canary in the superior's office; it may be a fern in the community room; or it may be a flea-bitten dog who haunts the kitchen door step.

In our house at Baguio in the Philippines, it was Tessie the cat, named after the great St. Teresa but not much like her in virtue. Tess had her kittens regularly under the house or in the laundry basket or on somebody's best habit. She knew our horarium to the minute. She never failed to leap to the first sound of the bell for the refectory, but chapel bells never broke her sleep. Everyone of us would have heard with joy that "that cat!" had been done away with; but do it ourselves? Ah no, poor Tessie wasn't as bad as all that.

In Hong Kong they have a dog who accepts you as one of the community only after several years' residence in the house and a lot of persuasive feeding. The Sisters construct elaborate barricades of school desks and portable blackboards every night to keep the all-too-zealous watchdog from making mincemeat of every visitor, either clerical or lay.

A cute little frog used to hop around the Kyoto garden and, from a tree outside, make his daily visit to the Blessed Sacrament through the chapel window. A real contemplative he was, spending hours with eyes unblinkingly fixed on the tabernacle.

But I met the most beloved pet of any convent I know, in Seoul, Korea, when the St. Paul de Chartres Sisters introduced me to Le Cheep.

Sister Eugenia arranged the meeting. She is one of three French Sisters in a community of 170 Koreans. My High School French does not extend much beyond, "Please pass the butter," and "Thank you," and I think Sister Eugenia could not even pass the butter in English. But my poverty in French was hardly noticeable, for "Oui, Oui" and "Merci" filled any space she left in the conversation. Any space she left at all, was purely by accident. And a more enthusiastic admirer of "Le Cheep" you could not imagine.

"Come," she said one afternoon, "come! Le Cheep will take us around Seoul. It is even now at the door, ma mere. Le Cheep is waiting for you." I didn't know who Le Cheep was, but certainly I would not keep him waiting.

There it stood—a jeep, and what a jeep! The chassis was blue, "blue for the Holy Virgin," Sister explained. The heavy wooden superstructure, a cross between a safe-deposit vault and a dog house, was bright yellow. The windows were small and awfully queer in shape. "But mon Dieu," exclaimed Sister, "what could we do? The glass was left from our very beautiful stained glass window. The children (very natural!) they break so many things! Yes, the glass is from that stained glass window, broken it is now many years.

"Look well, see here the hand of the Holy Virgin. We scrub very hard the glass, but no, the hand remains. There—there on the rear window, is the eye of La Sainte Vierge. Good, is it not," she concluded triumphantly, "that the Mother of God regards well the back where we cannot see for ourselves?"

The chauffeur, one of those indescribable convent handymen, opened the heavy wooden door with a heave-ho and a vast show of strength. The door would have done quite well on the great meat ice-box at the Maryknoll Seminary in New York. It must have been three solid inches thick. Indeed, as I stepped high into Le Cheep, I had the strange feeling that, instead of seats, there would be great hooks to hang oneself upon and I fancied I could feel the chill of death envelop my rigid frame. But Sister Eugenia was rattling on, displaying the beauties of her beloved cheep.

"See the door," she pointed out. "Of fine wood, and double the thick. So very frequent in the street comes the army truck. 'Out my way! Out my way!' the horn noises at all. But sometimes, it is not possible for out-the-way in time. 'So,' says Notre Mere (oh, she is wonderful in the head, our Notre Mere!) 'we will double-thick the doors and walls in Le Cheep.'"

The inside, oh the inside! The jeep had been lined with blankets and then covered with blue cotton cloth, ornamented with tiny roses and flowers. "Like the nightgown of my grandmere in France!" Sister Eugenia was quick to add. "My grandmere, she is dead now, but oh, so holy!"

Ceiling, wall, even the seats, were all blue cotton roses and flowers. Inside, Le Cheep was a gay little padded cell. "You see," said Sister, "very rough the roads and sometimes we must hold with both hands the seat. Even so, bop! and your head strikes the wall or ceiling. 'It is well,' says Notre Mere, 'that we put the stuffing over our heads and around us.' How wise is our Notre Mere!"

She saw me gaping at the thumbtacks of many colors which sprinkled the flowers, tacking the cotton and the blankets to the walls.

"You admire our tacks-for-the-thumb!" she was delighted. "At first we have the plain ones, silver only. It is not pretty, but we are poor religious, ma mere. What can we ask for in this here-below life? Must we have grandeur on earth and yet ask also for Heaven? Mais, non! But the Good God, He is ever mindful that we poor creatures love well the beauty. Ah, He is good. He arrange to break camp a unit of those so-good American soldiers near this place. Many things they are too lazy to pack up and take away. Comes the Colonel to us. 'You want these?' he asks and throws to us many boxes of these tacks-for-the-thumb. Ay, mon Dieu, we are so happy! You can see for yourself, ma mere; I do not exaggerate. See everywhere inside Le Cheep—

here red, here green, here gold, here yellow, here white. Like
stars, no? So elegant! Like stars of many colors set in the blue
of my grandmere's nightdress!"

We settled ourselves on the padded seats; the handyman let
that ice-box door slam upon us, and crawled into the front seat.
Sister Eugenia had one more suggestion.

"Ma mere, you will see our city! But let me suggest. First,
you will close one eye and rest it well. The windows—yes there
is much much room for one eye. But for the other, no. It is not
good for it to try to see through the hand of the Holy Virgin."

Thus I saw Seoul. I marvelled at the honored place in the
community this monstrous jeep enjoyed. Would you, in a big-
hearted moment, trade your Buick or your Cadillac for it? Ah no.
The Sisters of St. Paul de Chartres in Seoul would as soon trade
in the sainted grandmere herself, blue-flowered nightgown and
all, on an American model grandmere who wears pajamas.

Le Cheep took us sight-seeing, although I had to disengage
myself from the star-sprinkled interior to really see the sights.
We went to the Capitol Building—truly impressive. I climbed out
of the armored-car, and aimed my camera at one of the huge
stone dogs with glorious curly hair who guard the entrance.
Just when everything was nicely set, and the dog was grinning
at me through the view finder, his stone teeth bared, and white
tongue licking his voracious chops—just, as I say, I was ready to
add this to my views of the Orient, a hullabaloo arose from the
guardhouse. Two soldiers came tearing on, hollering in good old
Japanese fashion, and I gathered my skirts around me and de-
scended with great dignity to the rolling padded-cell, known as
"Le Cheep."

We also went to Tai Go Temple, the richest in Seoul. Here
I expected all sorts of restrictions, but the Buddhist priest required only that we take off our shoes. It was quite late in the
afternoon, but he opened windows and doors to enable me to
take a picture of the fantastic altar, the rich colored ceiling, the
shiny floor. It is all one room, at least forty feet high. Away up
there, monstrous gold, red, blue and green serpents in vivid
mottling, slide along the rafters and rear their heads with eyes
and teeth aglow. The rafters themselves gleam with gold leaf

and colors like jewels. A golden Buddha, at least 15 feet high, sits enthroned on the altar; lesser gods and goddesses form a painted but rhythmic background for the calm majesty of him— so placid, now that all desire has been purged. His twelve dignitaries, who propagated Buddhism throughout the nations are pictured on the walls in fantastic postures.

Then, the sturdy Cheep gathered his strength together and with here a rattle and there a pause for breath, brought us up to Nam San, or South Mountain, where the entire city of Seoul can be seen. One sees the hand of the Japanese here. A good road, a concrete balustrade, many seats to rest on, children buying gaudy candy at rolling stands, old people chatting under the trees, and, most indicative of all, the remains of a shinto shrine crowning the eminence at the top of a tremendous flight of stairs which scales the mountainside from the street far below. Odd, not a torii, not a shinto shrine, not even a Katakana character can be seen in Korea! They are trying to expunge completely, the Japanese chapter in Korean history.

I never saw a place where children were so beloved and so loving as in the St. Paul de Chartres Orphanage at Seoul. There are plenty to love, too—270 of them, all ages from a few days to 15 or 16 years old. You should see the Japanese house across the lane, where the babies are! It's like the famous old lady who lived in a shoe. The little chubbies topple unsteadily, and grab for support to the legs of the cribs where the babies sleep; the Sisters change the diapers and pause to pinch the cheeks and pull the button noses and talk baby-talk as they attend to more serious business. And when Sister Superior comes in sight! The Toddlers make a beeline for her, hold on to her skirts, put their arms tight around her knees and will not let her go. But La Superior is practical, oh very! She has several sheets of soft paper in that marvellous pocket of hers, and she sets to wiping noses like an old hand at the game.

Then she turns to me. "There are forty babies in the cribs. Some, pauvres petites, will not live. They are far too wasted before they are brought to the Sisters. Three or four arrive each day. Most are sent by the Government; not even the Sisters know the stories behind many. Some are brought by their mothers, poor women! They have had a good chance for marriage and do not wish to be embarrassed by evidence of previous affairs."

There are thirty who are advanced from plain babyhood. They are able to wobble here and there on their own two legs. These sleep on the immaculate floor of what was formerly "the house for the motorcar." Early in life, they learn to pack away their little sleeping-pads each morning, to bring out the small tables to the center of the room, and to place their own individual tiny chairs at the right place for the day.

The older girls have classes; they learn sewing and magnificent embroidery, as well as a fair schooling. True, they work hard—that is, hard for an American child, but certainly not for an Oriental poor child. Everybody works hard—Sisters, postulants, orphans. On Sunday mornings, you see a strange ballet. A string of chattering, merry dancers slide on pads down the gleaming corridor; Sisters, novices, orphans, "juvenistes" and house-girls holding hands to keep together in rhythm, having the time of their lives and getting the floor polished at the same time.

They play hard, too, these orphans. In the yard below my window, I silently refereed many a game with the athletic equipment American soldiers have given—good strong throwing, screaming laughter, and a jolly time for all. No supervised play, this; no indeed, just like the games of my youth when every child in our block used to gather under the street lamp in the summer evenings and we'd play Hopscotch, and Run-Sheep-Run, and Catch the Robber, and I Spy, without benefit, thank you, of anybody supervising our play.

While I was there an American Army truck rolled in with perhaps 40 sticky-wet cardboard cases. Before the dust had settled once more, Sisters, novices and older girls were hilariously busy. It was corn syrup in damaged cans. One set of girls had a dishpan and were washing the big #10 cans. Another group made holes in them. A third watched with glee the thick sweet stuff pour into large crocks and were not above sticking their fingers into the stream and licking them off. The strongest of all, carried the crocks to the storeroom. The little orphans, of course, were corn syrup from head to foot, as they roamed here and there getting a taste from anybody who would stop work long enough. There was just *too* much corn syrup, even for the big pottery crocks. Notre Mere gave the word, and everyone dashed into her proper building to get a cup and return for a treat of corn syrup drunk down just plain. And they *weren't* sick the next day, either.

In the orphanage at Seoul, there are many marks of the American occupation—some amusing, some tragic. Six muffins, all half-American, toddle unsteadily in the play yard. A little Negro with Korean eyes clung to my skirts when we made a tour of the orphanage. But there are better evidences than that. For instance, there are the crocks of corn syrup down in the storeroom; there are the 54 beds for the older girls placed in neat rows in one of the large dormitories; there are 60 more beds stacked on the back porch for the Sisters. The other day, 150 cases of milk came for the babies.

It was a pleasant surprise, too, to find good American coffee on my tray every morning. But most amusing of all—the holy water font in Notre Mere's office is a fancy cold cream jar put to good use at last. Mere Louise also keeps her needles in a former lipstick container. "Very simple," she says. "If you will but detach the red stuff, you will have a choice container for the needles."

These French Sisters! They would put the devil himself to good work and make a right handy fellow out of him!

19

Red Faces in Pusan

IT WAS strange to step off the plane at Seoul, Korea. They called it the Milk Plane, because the Americans of the ECA groups in Korea depend on it to get milk from the Army in Tokyo. Only natives and po' white trash like missionaries have to exist on canned milk in the Orient now.

It was strange, I say, because as the odd assortment of passengers lined up for immigration and customs inspection, I knew that I was the only Maryknoll Sister in the whole country.

But I didn't feel strange long. Outside the shabby room where we slowly shuffled forward in line, there arose a cloud of dust on the air field. And in the middle of it, a blue jeep bearing some 200 pounds of geniality in the person of Father George Carroll of New York and of Maryknoll. When the dust had settled a bit, there also came to view the stiff white headdresses of two French St. Paul de Chartres Sisters sitting with the dignity of French Grandes Dames in the back seat. I was to stay at their convent and they had insisted on being a reception committee with "le Pere Carroll."

From that time on, my guardian angel could go on vacation, for Father Carroll took over his work nicely.

Years ago, when Maryknoll was young, a curly haired chubby little fellow in the preparatory seminary in Pennsylvania, used to get around the Sisters time and time again, in the matter of two cookies instead of one, or an extra bit of ice cream for being a good boy. There are few of the older Sisters he does not know; and few of us who are not friends with Father George Carroll.

We were travelling one long day to Pusan, a port on the Southern tip of Korea only 8 hours by boat from Japan. The train was plainly a relic of former glory. The seats were ragged and dirty; the windows had not been washed since Pearl Harbor Day. Like European trains the aisle ran down one side of the car, past the doors of compartments for six or eight passengers.

We sat opposite one another and tried to say office. But Father Carroll had not seen a Maryknoll Sister for so long, he was dying for news. He put a pudgy finger to hold his place in his breviary and waited for me to finish a psalm.

"What ever happened to Sister Anthony?" he asked. "She used to be at the Venard years ago." I gave an account of Sister Anthony's doings and we again tackled our prayer books. Then,

"And Sister Philomena! My, she was strong! She used to turn the faucets off with such force, she wore out the washers. I'd like to have a nickel now for every faucet I fixed for her!"

It was a good old When-You-And-I-Were-Young session as the green hills and deep valleys, the rice fields and thatched huts of Korea passed by.

Maryknoll of the old days lived again. Days when the Sisters lived in many small farmhouses scattered over the compound; days when we entertained our guests under The Circle Tree on the lawn, because we didn't have room to do it inside; days of such hard work and such vigorous joy. The thrill when the early groups of priests and Sisters left for the missions; the hope that, someday, we might have 200 Sisters; the overwhelming happiness when in 1920 the 35 of us were recognized by Rome as a religious congregation. And threading like gold and silver through the recollections, were the memories of Father James A. Walsh of the keen eyes and kind mouth, and Mother Mary Joseph, leader and chief inspiration of the Sisters. We couldn't call either one by the titles they bear now. No, it was "The General" for the late Bishop James A. Walsh, Co-Founder of the Catholic Foreign Mission Society of America, known as Maryknoll, and just

"Mother" for our Mother Foundress, whom God still spares to her Sisters.

In Pusan, it was a great lift to see how the Church has come to town, literally, since the war. A solid old Japanese Shinto temple in the very heart of the city has been converted to a Catholic church and 1500 parishioners cluster around it. Formerly the only parish in Pusan was five miles from the city.

"When I first came here, several years before the war," a fine old Catholic gentleman told me, "nobody knew there was a Catholic church in the area. This Shinto shrine was well known, however. Now," he smiled triumphantly, "you would be hard put to find a Shinto shrine, but the Catholic church is right in the middle of town!"

Somewhere in the bleak swamps in the Land-Of-Fading-Gods, the great ones of Shinto have very red faces. Probably, they don't like even to hear the word "Pusan." For, where formerly dancing priestesses slithered across a polished floor and weird music wailed in honor of The-Gods-That-Are-Not, now altar boys carry book and bell to honor He-Who-Is in Holy Mass, and the incense of Catholic prayer ascends through the curving roof.

I stepped in to pray a bit one morning and found the Ladies' Altar Society in full brigade cleaning the church for tomorrow's Sunday Mass. Some thirty of those inexplicably cute Korean shoes, pointed like a canoe at the toe, were lined up before a great platform, which was really the entire church floor. Ashamed to see my big foreign clod-hoppers beside that dainty footwear, I went far to one side to remove them and walked with stockinged feet on the matting.

There were no pews, of course; one doesn't expect them in Korea or Japan. You choose your spot on the immaculate floor, sink to the ground on both knees and then sit back on your heels. It's simple, quiet, dignified. But you have to be born to it before you can call it comfortable.

I watched the ladies at work. Just like home! There was one who would do nothing but shine candlesticks, and another whose vigorous broom banged into every pillar in the place. On the whole though, they worked well together—an inspiration to the

foreign grey-clad Sister over by the wall. I understood not a word
they said, but I recognized every thought in their minds, for I
have cleaned many a church in my day. One bent old woman
must have crossed the aisle twenty times. It took her a minute
to touch one knee to the floor and another to rise, but she never
omitted the full genuflection, two minutes of reverence to God
before she went on with her work.

"And most of these women are converts of only a year or
so!" I thought. "It shows how the Church is One, even in non-
essentials. Here in Pusan, Korea, the Ladies' Altar Society is a
carbon copy of the one in my home parish."

Then we went to see the site of a hospital to be opened in
Pusan. (We did open it six months later.) The hospital building
was fairly big but the convent was a doll-house set like a gem
in a garden. At one time, it was the showplace of Pusan—not
that it was pretentious at all but the Japanese who owned it was
a gardening wizard. He must have spent little time indoors. The
house is tiny, one large room and two very small ones, just enough
to eat and sleep in and entertain an occasional guest or two. But
the garden stretches up the hillside in one level of beauty after
another. Even five untended years after the war could not ruin
its tangled vistas of sea and mountains.

We left the house and climbed up the garden's steep slope.
A grave dug into the hillside was sealed by a great black stone.
A frame of brass lamps surrounded it. The grave was not occupied, the Koreans told me. The owner had built it for himself
where he could rest forever in his beloved garden. Poor soul! He's
probably somewhere in Japan now, crowded into a city apart-
ment, glad to get a glimpse of a public park now and then.

We were standing on a large stone half sunk into the ground.
It was so big that it formed the entire foundation for a summer
house.

"You don't know what you're standing on," I was told. "This
is the largest single stone in the entire southern point of Korea.
This is how it got here.

"There was another garden enthusiast in Pusan who claimed
that he had in his garden the largest stone in all Southern Korea.

The man who built this garden wanted to take the title from him. So he searched all over Korea for a stone bigger than his rival's. At last he found it away up north—this one.

"He had quite a time getting it here. First it had to be dug from the earth. Then he had to build a special wagon to put it on, and construct a special road to get it to the railroad, with the help of 20 horses. Once near the railroad, a flat-top car had to be built. It was a ticklish engineering job to get the stone from the wagon to the car. At last, the thing was ready to travel to Pusan by rail. But here our friend ran into real trouble. The government refused to let it travel on the railroad because the bridges might break with such a load. It was only when the owner promised in writing to rebuild at his own expense any broken bridges, that permission was granted. Trestles along the route were bolstered up; every inch of track inspected. Then the monstrous stone rolled slowly down the Korean peninsula to Pusan.

"How he ever got it hauled half way up this mountainside, I can't imagine. But here it is, half buried again in mud washing down the hillside, and hardly anyone knows the bother it was to get here. But, for all that, it is the biggest stone in Southern Korea."

The former owner had been a devout Shintoist. A lovely little shrine, of succeeding steps and landings mounted to a stone-flagged level spot hemmed by cement seats and a balustrade. A perfect spot for the prospective patients to read and rest overlooking the harbor. A torii of stone arched the shrine and a pedestal was there for offerings.

Just to make the Shinto deities in the Land-of-Fading-Gods a little redder, I said, "What a perfect spot for a Lourdes shrine to Our Blessed Mother!"

In Korea I tried to get in touch with our Sister Agneta, then seven years alone in Northern Korea unable to rejoin her Mary-knoll community.

Sister Agneta was Mary Chang, a Korean of the highest type. Of an old Catholic family, she was a graduate of Sacred Heart College in Tokyo, a very exclusive school. At the time, she was the only Korean admitted. Her family has always taken a large part in the government. Her father is Chief of Customs at Pusan, Korea's largest port. Her brother Louis was formerly Minister of Education and is now head of the National University's art department, a well-known painter in both European and Korean styles, with long years of foreign education. John Chang was head of the Korean delegation to the United Nations and represented his country at Washington. He is now Premier. All are sterling Catholics.

In 1935 Sister Agneta was placed in charge of a religious congregation just then forming at Seoul, Korea. As a Maryknoll Sister, she was to train them to religious life. The war broke six years later and all the American Sisters were removed from their dispensaries, hospital and charitable institutions, sent into internment camps and later were repatriated. Sister Agneta was not permitted to go with them. Alone of her community, she remained at Pyongyang.

We all know what happened in those last days of the war. Russia swooped down on Manchuria and occupied most of it. The northern half of Korea went down her capacious throat, too. And with it, our Sister Agneta. A group of five others, three Japanese, one Korean and a German Sister were in a similar situation in Dairen, Manchuria. They were able to get out late in 1947.

All efforts to see Sister Agneta failed, whether the attempt was made from Free Korea where the Maryknoll Fathers were, or from Manchuria where our own Sisters had returned. Seoul is a matter of only five hours by train from Pyongyang, yet the heavy silence between them is appalling. Little news comes over the border. Once in a long, long time, we might receive a sketchy message through her brothers or father; but most of the time we prayed in ignorance of what she was undergoing.

Father Carroll tried three times to obtain a permit to cross the border into Communist-held Korea. Twice he heard nothing; the third time he got the answer, "The Reverend George Carroll will be an unwelcome guest in Northern Korea."

Nothing daunted, I also tried. But I never received an answer.

In the meantime, my stay in Korea was running out. It

seemed I should fail completely. Her own family had not received word in more than a year—ever since the American Liaison Group in Pyongyang was removed in December, 1948.

However, the night before I left, a strange thing happened. During the wee, sma' hours, the doorbell at the St. Paul de Chartres convent in Seoul pealed and pealed. Not too long after, the Mother Superior came to me.

"We have admitted a refugee Benedictine Sister from the North. She has news of Sister Agneta. Come."

A fairly young Korean woman lay on a bed in the Sisters' infirmary. Her working woman's clothes were arranged neatly on a chair beside her. She was resting on the pillow when we came in; the long lines of nervous tension and physical exhaustion showed plainly on her face. At the sight of me she raised herself in bed.

I certainly needed the Gift of Tongues then, and I didn't have it. The refugee became quite excited, babbling a mile a minute in Korean. She clung to my arm desperately. She sucked in her cheeks in an effort to show how emaciated Sister Agneta was. The Mother Superior translated her story into French, and as best I could I followed it.

This young Sister was a member of the great Benedictine monastery in Wonsan, away up north in Korea, next to Manchuria. About a month ago, the Communists had commandeered the buildings. The German Sisters who had been training the Korean community, were sent into concentration camps near Pyongyang. As for the Korean Sisters, the Communists merely took their habits from them and advised them to "do something useful with their lives."

This young Sister determined to get across the border and reach Seoul where she might be able to live her religious life. She travelled to Pyongyang and stayed there a few days resting with the Korean Sisters that Sister Agneta was training.

"The Communists hate her with a very special hate," she said. "They know that the Chang family fights Communism here and in America. They know, too, that she is a member of an American order. Her convent is near the concentration camp;

she feels them watching her all the time. Consequently, she rarely goes outside the building.

"Nevertheless, so far, the community is still permitted to exist. There are two houses in Pyongyang itself in different parishes and the Motherhouse is just outside the city.

"I slid across the 38th parallel by night and have been walking at night ever since. Even in Southern Korea, Red agents may track me down. But in a big city like Seoul, maybe I will be safe."

With this, she closed her eyes and her head nodded. Plainly, she should not be questioned any more. I loosened her grasp on my arm and lowered her gently back on the bed. She was asleep before her head rested on the pillow.

She was still sleeping when I slipped out of the house and took an early plane to Tokyo. And that was the last word anyone had of our Sister Agneta, for some time.

Then we heard of her death. It was sad but glorious. In the fall of 1950 when United Nations forces swept the Red Army back to Manchuria, Pyongyang was freed temporarily. Before the Reds evacuated the city, however, they took a truckload of women prisoners outside the city. Sister Agneta, ill at the time, was with them. They were all killed and buried in a ditch.

Sister earned her martyr's death on several counts—and all of them are worth dying for. Her family's strenuous activity against Communism was one. Her membership in an American religious order was another. The third was her own ardent Faith and her power to raise up women of God among her fellow Koreans.

The Communists indeed had a heavy score to even up with Maryknoll's Sister Agneta!

HAWAII

HAWAH

20

Bright Gateway

IN ONE-HALF hour I flew from Maui in a sort of aerial taxi (three passengers and the pilot) and spent twenty-four hours at the famous leper colony of Molokai—the most profitable twenty-four hours of my life. It's truly a Gate of Heaven, not only because the next move for most patients is into Heaven, but because it is so overflowing with supernatural joy. You can't imagine how happy the place is.

The northern shore of Molokai is fearsome. A sheer cliff, two thousand feet high, rises as a tremendous wall straight from the sea. I could not see what was on top, for our little plane buzzed along the side at only a thousand feet. Green though it was, and broken by wispy white ribbons as rivers fell over the edge down to the green-blue sea, you could not imagine a more formidable barrier. At one spot along this giant wall, a tongue of sand points out into the water, barely rising above the waves, and perfectly flat. The mighty wall behind has nothing to do with it and relaxes its austerity not an inch; the cliff is still the cliff. The tiny bit of land creeps humbly to that tremendous wall and dares rear itself no higher. This is Kalaupapa, the leper colony. In old days, a guard was stationed at the single trail which zigzags up the cliff; but now no one wants to escape.

Our plane settled on the coarse grass of the shore. Father

Patrick was waiting for us—Father Patrick who has known so many Maryknollers in Hawaii. He drove us the short distance to the convent, pointing out the cemeteries along the way. There are no less than five Catholic cemeteries, besides the Japanese-American, the Latter Day Saints (Mormons) and Protestant cemeteries. Missionaries in the colony are: two Mormon Elders who guide a flock of about thirty, a woman minister named Alice, and the nine Franciscan Sisters, four Sacred Hearts Brothers and Father Patrick. Most of the lepers are Catholics; many are converts since they came to the colony.

Like any Hawaiian town, Kalaupapa is a nest of white cottages, gorgeous bougainvillea and hibiscus, bright bird-of-paradise flowers and poster-paint blue sky. The main streets are paved well; there are several nice little stores; the white cottages which house the police department, the Board of Health, the Superintendent's office, etc., are marked with neat signs, else one would never suspect them of being public buildings. A craft shop window displays a candlewick bedspread and two lovely photographs of mountain and sea; no one would ever think that "crab hands" worked the bedspread and framed the pictures.

The Sisters' convent is also a white cottage set in green lawn, and surrounded as everybody's house is, by a neat picket fence. But the patients never step inside that fence. This is one of the few precautions the Sisters take. Even their chapel, a separate building on the convent grounds is half for them and half for the patients who have a special side entrance. There is a large church for the patients, but the Sisters share their chapel, nonetheless. Sister Martina, the Superior, warned us not to touch anything as we went around visiting the patients in their homes and in the hospital, but she and all the others were free in patting them on the shoulders, lifting their hands to show how the fingers had shrunk, and smoothing down their hair when the poor things were having trouble in keeping it tidy with their stumps of hands. It is a joy to know that they have the courage to treat these living corpses with kindly freedom. The Sisters rely absolutely on Mother Marianne's promise that, using normal cleanliness, none of her Sisters would ever contract the disease. None ever has.

Molokai is not the place it was in Damien's day sixty years ago, nor in Mother Marianne's last days, forty years ago, nor even what it was ten years ago. The sulfone drugs have made the difference. Whereas, formerly, there were a thousand or more lepers with running sores, horrible stenches, muffled in dressings from head to foot, there are now but two hundred seventy; fifty of these are "on parole," which means that they have been declared clean but prefer to remain on Molokai. They are too disfigured to be happy in ordinary society and too maimed to be able to earn a living. One sees now and then a patch of dressings here or there, an arm wrapped up, or a hand. But for the most part, the mutilated hands and faces and feet are healed and dry.

The first treatment given is Promine, intravenously, but this is very toxic and the patient is later given tablets of diazone, promizale, sulfatrone and Promecetin. The last is the best, but cannot be supplied in sufficient quantity. It's marvellous how these have contributed to the whole morale of the place since the patients are no longer made miserable with running ulcers.

"I used to be covered with white bandage—all my arms and hands and legs. It took hours to get the dressings changed every morning," one woman told me. "But now . . ." she rubbed her scarred stumps of hands up and down her brown arms to show the healthy flesh, puckered and furrowed though it was.

Many of the Sisters and other workers feel, however, that the new drugs may heal ulcers, but they definitely injure the interior organs. Sudden hemorrhaging and unexpected deaths have increased since they have been used. A Miss Lee, in the hospital laboratory, showed us leprosy bacilli under the microscope. "Nowadays, we rarely see a strong germ," she said. "It's plain that sulfone drugs destroy them. Indeed, it is a question in my mind whether, even though a case may still be active, the germs are strong enough to infect someone else." (Miss Lee is a fine Catholic girl; her absorbing interest in leprosy made her almost join the Marist Sisters because they have six leprosaria in the world. But her interest is more scientific than religious, although she is a daily communicant.)

Nearly everyone in the colony is undergoing "snipping."

This is a series of tests. Every month a bit of tissue is tested for germs; if the result is negative for four successive months, a deep cut is made and the tissue is sent to Honolulu for testing. After a week or so (what an anxious week!) the answer comes back. In that official white envelope is either exhilarating cleanliness, a reprieve from further decay, and freedom to live anywhere with but a check-up every three months—or failure and a year to wait before another try.

Beverly had a biopsy, or deep cut, and was sitting on the anxious seat right now. This is the drama of Beverly; she is sixteen, really a magazine cover girl. At eleven, she came to Molokai, to join her mother, also a leper, who has since died and is buried on Molokai. Her two sisters and three brothers live in Honolulu. If Beverly is pronounced clean, she can join them. There is not a visible scar on her; she wears pretty clothes; talks like any other bobby soxer; fixes her room like a college girl's. But when Beverly looks at you, you know that she has matured far beyond her sixteen years. I asked her what she was going to do with her life if the test is successful.

"Gee, I don't know, Sister," she said. "The thing I want most to do is closed to me. I want to help in an orphanage, to take care of children. But they'd never let me. I know—it wouldn't be right."

"Maybe you'll be taking care of your own," I said, trying to be sprightly.

"Maybe," she said shortly, and looked straight at me saying plainly with her eyes, "but who would marry me if he knew?"

Besides the use of new drugs, surgery has come to help the leper become more bearable to himself. In the old days, when the ear lobes enlarged so much, they hung down until they touched the shoulders. Now ears are trimmed to a decent size. Arms and legs are cut off before they fall off. When the mouth puckers so that one cannot get a spoon into it, it is slit at the corners; formerly, the Sisters say, several died of malnutrition simply because their mouths were too small even to force food into them. One man at the settlement has a plastic nose which fits nicely between the lenses of his glasses. Another has

Hawaiian harmony—composed of all nations and races.

HER CABBAGE PATCH ISN'T WORRYING GRANDMA SUZUKI IN
HAWAII; AN ERRANT GRANDSON BRINGS THESE TEARS.

FILIPINO WORKERS IN THE SUGARCANE FIELDS LIKE TO SHARE
AVOCADOS WITH THE SISTERS.

HAWAIIAN SCHOOLS ARE A CROSS-SECTION OF THE WORLD.

GERONIMO, A BAD HEART CASE, WINS THE GAME EVERY TIME—ALMOST!

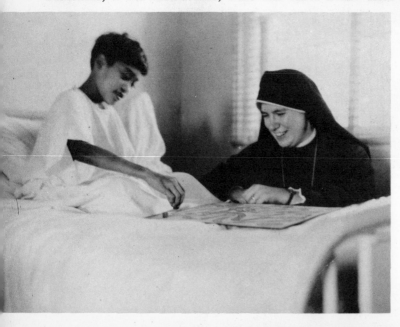

a bit of thumb made by splitting the old stump down to the wrist. Many are breathing through tubes in the throat. But of late the general health has so improved in eleven cases that the collapsed tracheae have opened again. Now, everyone has the hope of someday breathing normally.

I'll tell you some sad, sad stories now, but don't think for a minute that these are sad, sad people. As we went through the infirmary two hearty women, washing dishes in the sink, were having a wonderful laugh over something, both of them legless in wheelchairs and clutching the dishes between fingerless hands. Later, as we sat on the convent porch, two others swung around the convent driveway in a car and gave us a merry wave and hello. One is blind but has money; she bought a car. The other drives although she has only one leg and her fingers are gone. "I thank Our Lord for letting me find out ways to get around and help myself," she says. "I aim to stay independent as long as I can."

Lelani is all but blind, has no fingers and breathes through a tube. She must stop the hole in her throat with her poor hand every time she wants to say something. Yet every remark is a quip or an expression of gratitude. "We're all so happy here," she says, "and why not? We have Our Lord in the Blessed Sacrament, and the Sisters, and our sodality and Holy Name societies. Everybody is so kind, so I say, who's better treated than we are?"

Henry is a former Army boy and the sulfone drugs are having little effect on him; his face is swollen horribly and he has "the bumps" on arms and legs. But he says, "I'm twenty-six and the best years of my life have been here; this is where I learned to live." You should see him playing with his dog, Thunder, rolling and laughing, wrestling and growling on the ground. He is one of Sister Patrice's boys, a convert and daily communicant.

There is buoyancy in Molokai, a bright, simple joy, and I think it springs from depths beneath as all supernatural joy does.

We spoke of Beverly; Winifred is her chum. The two could pose as American and Hawaiian beauties. But Winifred is far from gaining her freedom. Just this morning, she carelessly left her hand on the sterilizer as the doctor was dressing a sore. Her hand is numb, of course, and the flesh was cooked before Winifred realized what had happened.

Josephine is only eighteen, but she is far from beautiful. Her face is paralyzed; the great heavy cheeks and lips hang grotesquely. Her food is served to her in shallow dishes and she laps it up like a dog with her tongue. If there is anything solid, she throws her dead clumps of hands against her lower jaw again and again to make a pretense of chewing.

Ethel has been blind thirty-seven years; that's how leprosy started with her. She came to Molokai twenty-three years ago. Just last year she obtained special permission to go by plane to Maui where she might talk to her mother but not disembark from the plane. She was quite excited about it, but on the day before, a letter came from her sister—bitter words about insinuating herself into the family again. Did she not know, they would all be stigmatized, their business ruined, if they were recognized at the airport? Ethel felt it keenly, but perhaps it is just as well her mother cannot see her now. Her eyes are removed, her nose has fallen back into her face, her feet and hands are insensible, fingerless clumps, her eyebrows are gone and her hair (that dank, lifeless hair of leprosy) has retreated halfway across her head.

She spends most of her day in the Sisters' chapel, when she is not puttering around her room setting things to rights. Usually she is at Mass every morning, but this morning it was raining. After all, when one must walk on stumps of feet and feel the way with a cane, it's a bit hard to hold an umbrella on a blustery day with fingerless hands as well. But bright and cheerful? "The Lord is so good to me; He has left me my voice. So I sing in our choir, praising Him and thanking Him for the Sisters, the Hospital, this beautiful place and praying for everybody I know." (I enlisted Ethel to pray for all the Maryknoll Ethels; Sister Marie and I are the only benefactors I know!)

May is lots of fun. She was fourteen when first afflicted. Later she and Joe escaped from the Kalihi Receiving Station, were married and made their way to Molokai—so anxious were they to get to the colony. Their boy Joseph and later the twins, Mary and Cecilia, were born at Kalaupapa; all three are now at

Mother Marianne is buried in a plot near the convent; Father Damien's grave is just as it was before the body was transferred to Belgium; Brother Dutton lies near it with the Sacred Hearts Fathers and Brothers who have worked on the island, in the same little cemetery beside Father Damien's Church. Kalawao is deserted now; the colony clusters at Kalaupapa. A few horses, owned by the lepers, graze outside the low stone wall; the blue ocean breaks in white along the shore; bougainvillea and hibiscus brighten the old grey frame church. The wind they loved blows through the rustling coconut trees. May they rest in peace—those holy bodies urged to such giant strides by the charity of Christ!

21

Missioners — Assorted Lots

ONCE upon a time there was a nice, big, good-natured elephant who put up very peaceably with a flea who lived in his ear. One day, as the elephant stepped off a trembling bridge, the flea cocked up his head and threw out his chest and said:

"My, we certainly made that bridge shake, didn't we?"

That's the way I feel about Maryknoll. It seems incredible now that there were hardly a dozen Americans on the mission field in 1918, and they were all members of European religious orders. It was in that year the first Maryknollers stepped on the soil of China and set about curling their tongues around Chinese words. Yet it is so.

In 40,000 miles you can see a lot of mission work, and I did. Mostly, of course, I saw Maryknollers in action, but I also came across the New York Jesuits in Palau, the Detroit Capuchins on Guam, and the North Carolina Mercy Sisters also on Guam; three American Ursulines in Swatow, the Notre Dame Sisters in Japan and tons of others. Indeed, there's hardly a spot on this globe now where a fellow-American priest, Brother or Sister won't rush forward to take your suitcase and ask if you like your eggs hard or soft-boiled. They'll ask you, even though they have no idea where to get the eggs.

Like the flea in the elephant's ear, I was carried along by folks who were grateful to America for sending Christ's emissaries to them. It was heartwarming to feel the gratitude of the people who repaid to me the debt of kindness and help they felt due to our missionary priests, Brothers and Sisters.

It was Pedro in Manila who began the process. He's a wizened up little fellow, who has been meeting boats in Manila harbor for 60 years, he says. He comes out with the Public Health inspector's boat, and scouts around to see if any Maryknoller is on board. As soon as he spots the habit, you might as well give up any notion of independence. Pedro piles your baggage where it ought to be; tells the customs and health officials that there is a Maryknoll Sister aboard and she ought to go to the head of the line for inspections. He has even been known to pilot the Public Health boat to our ship first when many others were waiting. Half the time he's busy about many odds and ends in getting you off; the rest of the time he bores you to tears talking about the marvellous Maryknoll Sisters.

In Canton, I was at the tender mercies of Maryknoll's Father O'Neill who will move mountains if he thinks you want them shoved aside for some reason. He careened us through the streets, almost deserted in the hurly-burly of Communist occupation, to the customs, the airport, the freight agent and to the Maryknoll Fathers' house.

In Swatow, three American Ursulines took us in. They had arrived a year before, one from Brooklyn, one from Illinois and one from California, knowing not one word of French or Chinese. But living with a French community and in a Chinese city has made them fairly proficient in each. Maryknoll Sisters pass through Swatow so frequently on their way to the interior, that the Ursulines built a little addition to their convent, which they call the Maryknoll Suite, to accommodate us enroute.

One of the Sisters was chatting with us at breakfast; she kept urging us to take the butter. "Oh, do have some more butter," she said again and again.

"You're very anxious to get rid of that butter," I observed.

"It's *so* good," she sighed, "and I know you will appreciate it. It's Brooklyn butter; my brother sent it to me and we have been saving it for the next Maryknollers to come through from the interior missions."

There are now 566 American priests and Sisters in China, a good advance over the picture 25 years ago, but still only a very small percentage of the number of European missioners. One-third of these are Maryknollers, 139 priests and 63 Sisters. Besides the missions in the interior, American Catholic missioners are exerting great influence in large port cities. Bishop James E. Walsh in Shanghai, the five young Maryknollers who teach in Lingnam University in Canton (which started out as a Protestant college), and our own big Maryknoll Convent School in Kowloon, one of the most beautiful buildings in the Hong Kong area, where 700 girls are being trained to Catholic ways of thinking.

I had one of the most gratifying weeks in years in Tokyo. Here we stayed at the Catholic Club up on the 7th floor of the Mitsikusi Department Store on the Ginza, which is the great Tokyo shopping center. It was strange to enter the store from the street, pass among the counters reading their quaint English signs ("tranks" for trunks), elbow your way into the elevator with the other shoppers and then step off at the 7th floor to a quiet foyer before the chapel.

Here lives Father Tibesar, who has become more or less a legend in Maryknoll. He is the head of Catholic Charities in Japan; he runs the Catholic Club where 200 people are constantly under instruction in the Faith; he is a great mountain of a man from Quincy, Illinois, with more energy and bright ideas than a dozen lesser men. He offered to let us stay at the club while in Tokyo for we Sisters have no house in the city.

As I mentioned earlier, Japan right now is packed with all her citizens who formerly lived in Manchuria, Korea, China, the Philippines and Pacific Islands—wherever their industrious merchants had set their stores or worked their plantations.

At the Catholic Club, we had old-home-week with many of these repatriates. A crowd of women and girls collected to see Maryknoll Sisters again. Two of them had been students at our Academy in Dairen, Manchuria; another one, smart, clever and thoroughly Americanized, had been at the Los Angeles school when she was little, had spent the war years with us in the Philippines and now was working for the American Army in

Tokyo. Tsuki San, with great sad eyes, had been baptized in Manchuria through the influence of our Sister Jean. Now, she told us how her parents had both died of the hardships attendant on their repatriation in a cattle-boat, waiting for days in a flimsy barracks in the depth of a Manchurian winter for the wretched boat to come. "But they asked for Baptism, Sister; each one wanted to die a Catholic. For that, I am glad."

We went to a tuberculosis hospital on the outskirts of the city with Father Kaschmitter (yes, another Maryknoller who runs the Tosei News, the Catholic News Service of Japan). Our purpose was to see a young girl, the youngest of a Seattle family which had gone to Manchuria to act as catechists there. Elizabeth, looking wan but oh, so glad to see Sister Hostia once more, outlined the family doings. "Joe died in the Southwest Pacific," she said. "Joe was the boy we all hoped would be a priest." How many girls in the States, I thought to myself, could say exactly the same sentence for an American soldier!

This hospital is fascinating. It is conducted by the Sisters of St. John the Evangelist—an all-Japanese, all-medical order. The Mother Superior and Foundress showed us through it. She wears a Sister's veil, white starched wimple, and a simple black Japanese kimono. She takes the sprinting cup for Sisters. Never seeming to walk fast, or even to be moving at a normal rate, nevertheless she was in and out of doors, up and down stairs and zipping along corridors until I was breathless in pursuit.

One time, I lost her. She had disappeared around a corner ahead and I paused outside the open door of a room to decide which way she had gone. Then I heard the cry inside the room.

"Maryknoll! A Maryknoll Sister."

It was a young man, half-raised from the bed in his excitement, who held out his hand to me. I went in to take his hand and he lay back panting from the exertion. Breathing hard, he told me the simple tale of how he knew Maryknoll.

"I was a cadet in the Japanese Navy 13 years ago. Part of our training was to sail from port to port on a sort of good-will tour. I was the only Catholic on board. When we got to Seattle, I left the ship to find a Catholic Church. It wasn't long before I wan-

dered into Star of the Sea Church, the Maryknoll Japanese
Mission in Seattle. The priest and Sisters made quite a fuss over
me and I was thrilled.

"Then we went to Hawaii and stopped at the island of Maui.
Here, too, I looked for the Catholic Church. Here, too, I met
the Maryknoll Sisters for one afternoon. I remember we all sat
under a big tree on the lawn; it was the most wonderful few
hours on that trip. At the end, one of the Sisters took me to see
a Japanese girl, blind and suffering from TB, who had just been
baptized a few days before. She was lying as I am now, finding
it hard to get enough breath. 'Please pray for me' she said, and I
promised. I've prayed so often for her since, Sister. She must be
dead now, but I still pray for her soul. I think of her so often
now, that I wonder if she is not watching me from Heaven,
helping me to bear the same sickness. I pass her request on to
you, Sister; pray for me."

I was afraid he would overtax himself—he was quite exhausted now. I hoped that Mother Superior would come to find
me. With the thought, she came swiftly into the room and ex-
pertly extricated me from his handclasp. But still he insisted on
naming the Sisters he met on Maui for one afternoon 13 years
ago—Sister Beata, Sister Francis Xavier, and so on. He remembered each one.

The Sisters of St. John the Evangelist have a fascinating
history. They were founded by a brilliant doctor, one who had
the honor of receiving his diploma from the hand of the Emperor
himself. He took post-graduate work in Europe and there became
a Catholic and later, a priest.

He died in 1938, a comparatively young man, but not before
he founded this order for Japanese medical women. Mother Superior is a doctor, and, among the nine professed Sisters, there
is another doctor, several nurses and a laboratory technician.
After living through the war years, the order seems now destined
for a period of growth. Already they are thinking of expanding
into "Mission houses" in other regions.

In Korea, it was the same story. Here I was under the kindly
wing of Father George Carroll of New York City and of Mary-

knoll, in charge of LARA distributions of relief. A horde of the miserable surround his little house behind the Cathedral. So little is it, that for Father Carroll to sleep he must pull his bed down from the wall, and then nobody can get in the front door.

One Sunday there, I tucked my missal underarm and thought I would take in an extra Mass at the Cathedral. Mass had begun, and, as I approached, it was plain that I would not be able to get inside. The door, the portico and the landing outside were filled with people craning their necks to get a view of the priest on the altar. No one paid much attention to me so I stood and craned, too, choosing some nice short women to peer over.

One of the women turned around. "Oh!" she exclaimed and touched her two companions. The Mass was forgotten for the moment. They took my hand and caressed my clothes, babbling all the while in Korean. I caught the names of some of our Sisters who had been in Northern Korea before the war.

We were really a major distraction to the pious faithful, so we hushed for the rest of the Mass. But they didn't let go of my hand nor of my habit. Right after Mass we hurried over to Father Carroll's house for a translator.

It was seven years since they had seen the Sisters off for repatriation in 1942. They had known our Sisters in Peng Yang, at the dispensary and old folks home in Gishu, in the mission house at Shingishu. They rattled off names so fast I couldn't jot them down quickly enough. Then one opened her prayerbook and handed me an aged photograph. Discolored though it was, I recognized the faces of six or seven of my confreres of Maryknoll.

That's Sister Luke—oh so jolly. And that's Sister Sylvester, how tall she was! And Sister Rose of Lima, the nurse. "But Sister, who is this? For years we have tried to identify her."

I didn't have much to work on. Only an eye and eyebrow showed behind the shorter Sister in front. Whoever she was, she was a modest violet. Her identity remains one of the great unsolved mysteries of our community, something like that of "the Murphy girl from Boston." This legendary character haunts me. Every now and then some dear old soul stops me on the street, or in a railroad station, usually just as I hurry for a train, to ask:

"Can you tell me where Sister—well I can't think of her name now but she was the Murphy girl from Boston. From St. Ignatius parish, I think, or perhaps from St. Patrick's. At least, I know she used to attend Mass once in a while at either of those churches. She entered Maryknoll about 15 years ago, or dear me, was it earlier than that? I remember meeting her at her aunt's house just a short while before one of my grandchildren was born. Now, could it have been Bobby or little Helen? Anyway, she's been a Maryknoll Sister for a good long time. And her aunt's name is Mrs. Murphy, but I couldn't be sure if that's her mother's sister or her father's. That would make a difference in the name, wouldn't it! Well, I won't hold you up a minute longer, Sister; you Sisters are all so busy and doing such a wonderful work. But do tell that Murphy girl from Boston that her dear old friend was asking for her."

Another of the pleasures of Seoul was getting to know Bishop Patrick J. Byrne, Apostolic Nuncio to Korea. (I'm truly sorry to mention so many Maryknollers, but of course tribal unity brought me knocking on their doors first.)

You can judge of Bishop Byrne's episcopal dignity by the fact that he refers to himself as "My Excellency, Uncle Pat." Tall, spare, with gently serious eyes and a mouth that cannot keep from uttering one dry quip after another, he is a man of legend among us. He was one of our first missioners in Korea, 25 years ago, and there picked up his mascot, a duck wearing the high hat of a Korean scholar. This duck, for years, was his trademark, appearing under his signature in every informal letter he wrote to Maryknoll. Most of us are a bit disappointed that he did not rate a place in the episcopal coat of arms. But certainly, he is engraved on the episcopal heart of "My Excellency, Uncle Pat."

For many years before the war, the then Father Byrne was in Japan. He was the only American not interned during the war, nor sent home on the repatriation ship, *Gripsholm*. When MacArthur set up his headquarters in Tokyo, Father Byrne was often called upon as an advisor who knew and understood the Japanese people. He went to Korea after the war as Papal Legate and in June, 1949, was consecrated by Bishop McDonnell, then National Director of the Society for the Propagation of the Faith in the United States.

Bishop Byrne's house was next door to President Rhee's. Father Craig and I swung into his driveway in a jeep, just as the Bishop was swinging out in his Chevrolet. "Go in and make yourselves at home," he called. "Mrs. So-and-So just telephoned that she can give me a head of lettuce, and lettuce in this country is worth going after. I'll be back in five minutes."

We waited a half-hour until the Apostolic Delegate returned with his head of lettuce.

Bishop Byrne and Father Booth, his secretary, are Maryknoll casualties of the Korean war. They were captured by the Reds in Seoul and marched from the city toward the north. An aged French priest, more than eighty years old, and a French St. Paul de Chartres Sister (my hostess in Seoul) were also in the line of march.

The half-frozen line of starvelings tottered out the north gate of Seoul. To where, no one knows. In all the fighting back and forth in Northern Korea, no trace has been found of Father Booth or of "My Excellency, your Uncle Pat." However, wherever he is, in this world or the next, I am sure his gently serious eyes regard the world with kindliness and his episcopal hand is raised in blessing over all, even (indeed, most particularly) over his persecutors.

In Hawaii, the fruit of 24 years' work was blessedly evident. When I first went to Hawaii in 1936 as a teacher, my classroom wasn't so bad, I thought. Indeed it was a distinct improvement on the buildings they started with 9 years before. But now, when I see the substantial brick school of three capacious floors, the linoleum, the scrumptious blackboards, I claim to be a pioneer. My little old classroom had no glass in the window openings; chicken wire across the place where glass should be, tried to discourage any thief who might hanker for my textbooks or my goldfish. But it didn't discourage the wind or the rain in the least. In a storm, we all merely crowded into the dry half of the room and watched the puddles on the wet half disappear through the cracks in the floor. Those cracks were very convenient. Sweeping the floor was simple; all the dirt fell through the cracks to the ground two feet below. There was never anything to pick up in a dustpan when you were finished.

One day when I was new to Hawaii I was teaching typing with ten typewriters banging away. "Is this an earthquake?" I asked the children. "It's the first one I've felt, but I understand you have them pretty often here." The poor boys and girls were mystified. They stopped typing and stared at me. With that, I knew; my earthquake was only the floor shaking to the tune of ten typewriters.

My old classroom has been painted white now. Fitted with glass windows and moved a bit closer to the convent, it serves quite nicely as an outside laundry.

In my day, there were five Catholic schools in Hawaii, manned by Maryknoll Sisters. Many of our children were non-Christians who had no idea of Christ, sons and daughters of simple pagans who had come from Japan, China, Korea, Samoa, and a thousand other little islands around. The Belgian Sacred Hearts Sisters had an Academy in Honolulu, the Franciscans from Syracuse had a struggling hospital in Honolulu, the Leper Hospital on Molokai, and a school at Hilo.

In the 14 years since then, five other groups of Sisters have come to maintain Hawaiian parochial schools in Honolulu and the other islands. Our own Maryknoll Sisters have increased 50%. Marianist Fathers and many more Maryknoll Fathers as well as the original Belgian Sacred Hearts Fathers who started the Catholic Church work in Hawaii in 1820, staff the parishes.

Hawaiian Catholicity is burgeoning. Brand new schools have been built here, and rooms added there. New works like Social Service and the training of lay teachers for Christian Doctrine classes in public schools are swinging along at a great rate. The Franciscans' hospital is a perfect dream with big buildings, expert medical equipment—all that a Supervisor longs for. Now that Hawaii is only 12 hours by air from "the mainland" as they call the United States, with planes buzzing in and buzzing out of the great new airport, it's no problem at all to go back and forth.

And yet, only 23 years ago when our Sisters first came, they slept for months on the school auditorium stage waiting for a convent to be built. It was an overnight trip by boat to Maui, where one now flies in little more than an hour. We cared for the Catholic children in our schools and filled in with hundreds of others; now even with doubled enrollment and the opening of many new schools, we cannot find room even for all the Catholic children.

So let us end this monologue of a travelogue on a cheerful note—cheerful, but not too blithely optimistic. This is no time to slacken at the oars but we can be glad that America is slowly taking her place among the great missionary nations of the world. She has a long, long way to go, however, before she can rival little Holland. No less than 6,512 Dutch missioners are in the field to represent her 3,600,000 Catholics. America's 26,700,000 will have to send to the fields afar 21,000 priests, 7,000 Brothers and 14,000 Sisters, more than ten times as many as they do now, before she can equal that percentage of vivid Faith. At present there are only 4,123, 5% of the total. Europe still supplies 90% of the 80,000 world foreign missioners; with Canada and Australia sending almost as many as we do, we supply the other 10%.

And yet American missioners have an advantage no others enjoy. The world is looking to America for leadership. Asia particularly hangs on our words with flattering attention. It is the dream of every Oriental to come to the States, at least to study, if not to live. Asia is all eagerness to learn our mechanics, to wear our clothes, to see our movies and to dance to our music. How much more important for them, if they could learn to know and love our God!